Jingle in my Pocket Book

Interactive Songs, Poems, Charts, and Games

PreK through 2nd Grade

by Sharon MacDonald

Grasshopper Press
15215 Chalet Drive
San Antonio, Texas 78232

This book is dedicated to my aunt, Frances Shuler Griffin, who has been such a large part of my life for as long as I can remember. She still is.

Editor: G. T. Nave
Illustrator: Sharon MacDonald

Entire contents Copyright © 2002 Grasshopper Press. However, the individual purchaser of this book may reproduce designated materials for the classroom and for individual use. The purchase of this book does not entitle reproduction of any part for an entire school, a district, or a school system. Such use is strictly prohibited.

ISBN 0-9705949-2-5

Table of Contents

Introduction	1
1 Jingle in My Pocket	12
2 Stack Up the Blocks	20
3 What the Animals Said!	25
4 What Can You Do?	31
5 Multi-plenti-cation	35
6 Caterpillar	40
7 Five Round Pumpkins	48
8 Shuffle, Bend, Slide, and Wave	56
9 Little Tree House	59
10 I Can't Spell Ohio	64
11 Triangles, Bells, Sticks, and Maracas	71
12 Fruit Salad	75
13 Scissors' Song	82
14 What's On A Face?	87
15 Barefoot's What I Choose!	91
16 Where is Africa?	96
17 Streamer's Song	100

What is Interactive Learning?

Interactive learning is what happens when a child is involved directly in an activity, learning by doing. It is a two-way process: The child acts on the activity; the activity elicits a response from the child. The child has choices to make. The interaction adds to the child's storehouse of knowledge. In the interactive model, children are active participants, not spectators.

The activities in this book have been designed to get the children involved. They teach the skills and concepts young children need to learn. Most of the activities can be self-directed. Some examples of self-directed activities are oral and written language exercises that ask the children to find words and letters, or to fill-in a word in a line of poetry.

Interactive learning is best achieved by using multiple-sensory channels--like seeing, hearing, touching, smelling, tasting, and singing. Information stored in this way is more easily retained and retrieved later. If children can hear, touch, sing, and read a word, for example, they learn it; and they will retain it for a long time. Let's look at learning the word **rough**, for example. If a child *felt* sandpaper, as well as *listened to, read,* and *sang* the word rough, the child would know what rough meant; it would be unlikely that he would ever forget it. Using two sensory channels to impart information is good; using three is optimum. It is not such a hard thing to add a component to an activity you are doing already to make it interactive. For example, you can match words, highlight letters, or add physical movement to any learning experience.

The Children Do Something With the Materials

Interactive means that the children *do something* with the materials. It means they help write stories and share them; record "research" results; move around puzzle pieces, and feel the texture of objects. *Interactive* work is a constructive, positive process, taking place in a structured setting. It is not in itself noisy or confusing. In summary, children gather information more easily, and they retain more completely, when they:

>Touch, feel, and fiddle with things,
>Move things around using their hands, feet, and bodies,
>Sing, chant, listen, and repeat words and phrases; and,
>Twist, stir, taste, and smell.

Reading skills can be taught interactively, also. Since learning to read is among the most important goals of early education, teaching reading interactively broadens the reading experience for the child. There are other skills, too, like math, writing, listening, spelling, and oral language that can be taught using interactive methods. We will have more on that later.

Let's look at an example of the effectiveness of interactive learning from our collective pasts. Remember *Mickey Mouse?* Can you spell it? Spell it. How did you do it? Sing it? Sure. Because you learned it as a song, and sung it often, *Mickey* is much easier to spell than, say, *Donald Duck?* What a powerful way it was to learn to spell.

The interactive possibilities of writing are different. Writing itself is *interaction.* What is missing for the child is a **reason** to write. On the following page is a list of the ways you can give the children a reason to write.

- Make a grocery list
- Share the pen among the children during morning message
- Add something to the "Must Do" class list
- Write a note to a friend
- Document their "scientific" research
- Label block constructions
- Create a menu
- Write a class thank you note
- Make signs
- Write a story to share with others
- Write down pretend phone messages
- Write important events on a calendar
- Tell how to make a peanut butter and jelly sandwich
- Describe their drawings and pictures
- Make a big book
- Write a get well card to a relative or friend
- Write on your "Remember to Bring it to School" list
- Write pumpkin words on a pumpkin with a *Visa Visa*

The battle for you will be in getting the children excited about writing; half the battle is won if they write about things that are important to them.

We have talked about using interactive activities to teach reading. We can use them to help teach math, as well. The following poem and activity are examples of math, but they still have the reading and listening components. The activity shows you how to make this poem interactive, or any other poem you select. If you do several things to the same poem, song, or story, you will cut down the number of interactive charts you need to make.

Five Round Pumpkins*
By Sharon MacDonald

Five round pumpkins
In a road side store
One became a jack-o-lantern
And then there were four.

Four round pumpkins
As orange as can be
One became a pumpkin pie
Then there were three.

Three round pumpkins
With nothing fun to do
One was cooked as pumpkin bread
And then there were two.

Two round pumpkins
Basking in the sun
One was cooked as pancakes
Then there was one.

One round pumpkin
One job was left undone
So he was kept to make new seeds
Then there were none.

*From <u>Everyday Discoveries: Amazingly Easy Science and Math Activities Using Stuff you Already Have</u> by Sharon MacDonald, published by Gryphon House.

Put the poem on a chart with a piece of soft-side Velcro placed below each number word. Write the number words and the numbers "1," "2," "3," "4," and "5" on short sentence strips. Put a small piece of hook-side *Velcro* (or sandpaper) on the back of the numbers and the number words. Have the children put either the number word, or number itself, below each number word. Please see Activity 7 for more ideas.

Interactive learning gives us a way to:

- Attract children to print
- Make work *relevant to the children's experiences*
- Allow children to work at their own ability level
- Help the children see themselves as readers
- Have the children review the skills they have learned
- Encourage the children to practice what they have learned
- Learn to problem-solve other ways of working with materials
- Work independently
- Assume more responsibility for some aspects of their own learning
- Assess the learning taking place continuously
- Work cooperatively with others
- Use poems, songs, chants, jingles, and sayings to invite the children to participate

Children need to acquire specific skills to be successful readers. The skills are listed below. Activities to build these skills need to be repeated over-and-over again. Repetition builds skills. Using interactive games, materials, and equipment, makes repetition fun; and creates new avenues to successfully re-teach and review previously learned skills.

(Note: The skills list on the following page focuses on literacy only; other curriculum areas would invite a list of different skills. Most curriculum concepts can be taught interactively, using many of the ideas presented in this book.)

Literacy Skills Learned Through Interactive Activities

- ✓ Directionality
- ✓ Letter recognition
- ✓ Rhyming words
- ✓ Root words
- ✓ Vowel sounds
- ✓ Beginning- and ending sounds
- ✓ Beginning- and ending blends
- ✓ Punctuation
- ✓ Spacing
- ✓ CVC
- ✓ CVCE
- ✓ One-to-one correspondence
- ✓ Differences between letters and words
- ✓ Letter formation
- ✓ Onset and rime
- ✓ Prefix and suffix
- ✓ Diagraphs
- ✓ Diphthongs
- ✓ Contractions
- ✓ Syllabication
- ✓ Vowel patterns
- ✓ Alliteration

How to Make Activities Interactive

There are many ways to make interactive materials; take a skill or a concept you want to teach and put it,

in:

A book of movable parts
A folder game
A pocket chart
Resealable bags
A pizza box or shoebox
Baskets, buckets, tote trays

on:

Charts and posters
An old game board
An overhead
A magnet- or flannel board
A bulletin board
A dry-erase marker on board
Pizza circles

To make the pieces moveable use:

- ✓ Brads
- ✓ *Velcro*
- ✓ *Sticky Tac*
- ✓ Magnetic strips
- ✓ Vinyl covers
- ✓ Removable hooks
- ✓ Paper clips
- ✓ Clothesline and pins
- ✓ Two-sided tape
- ✓ Highlight tape
- ✓ *Wikki Stix*
- ✓ Correction tape
- ✓ Notebook rings
- ✓ Rubber bands

Teach the Children to Use the Activities Successfully

Here are a few tips to teach the children to use the materials successfully:

- ✓ Make the activity self-checking. It does not matter if the child peeks at the answer. Working and reworking the activity is what reinforces learning.

- ✓ Put the activity in a low-traffic area. The children will work with less distraction there. It does not have to be a large area, just in an out-of-the-way place.

- ✓ Make the system self-managing by limiting the number of children using the activity at the one time. Let's take an example. Let's assume you want to limit the number of children using an activity to two. Place a library pocket nearby the activity. Have all the children's names on jumbo craft sticks; store them in an orange juice can. Write "2" on the pocket (the "2" means that only two children can work there). When a child wants to work the activity, he removes his name from the orange juice can and places it in the library pocket. When there are two sticks in the pocket, the activity is full.

 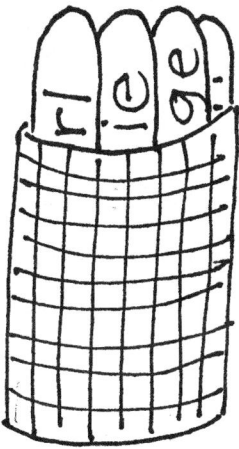

- ✓ Change an activity when you observe that most of the children are misusing it. It usually means that they are bored with it. Put out something new. When an activity is not being chosen, put it away. Take it out six weeks later. The children will like seeing an "old friend"; others will be ready for it that were not ready for it six weeks earlier.

Teach the Children to Work Independently

Train the children to use an activity successfully. Let's use a poem chart as an example; let's focus on keywords (keywords are the words you want the children to learn to read, to say, and to recognize). So, what do you need to do for the children to be successful? Here's a sequence.

- ✓ Read and re-read the poem aloud with the group until all the children know it.

- ✓ Move from the spoken words to pictures of keywords; pictures of what the words are describing. If the word says "apple," for example, have a picture of an apple. Display the poem chart. The children will associate the word with a picture of it.
- ✓ Once the children know the poem and the keywords, move to written words of the picture. Set the pictures aside; have the children match the written words to keywords in the poem. Have them place the written words over the keywords in the poem.
- ✓ When the children understand matching the written word to the keywords in the poem, cover the keywords with masking tape; have the children find the keywords written on cards and place them in each "missing word" spot in the poem.
- ✓ Model how to move the words and the sentence segments on the poem chart. This builds interest and enthusiasm. The children observe how to do the poem chart successfully. The children themselves become models for the other children. They will show each other.
- ✓ Have several of the children model how to use the moveable parts of the poem chart. Let them show what they know. You'll find out if they really do understand how you expect them to use it. Such insights are especially useful when you are occupied in another corner of the room while they are working with interactive stuff elsewhere.
- ✓ Place the poem chart in an independent work area for the children. They really will do it all by themselves.

How to Store All of the Interactive Stuff

Storage is a universal problem for teachers. There is no easy solution. For small things, I have found that copy-paper boxes work well. Label the contents, or the topic, in an easy-to-see place. That way, you won't have to take the boxes down to know what's inside them. Write a more detailed contents list on the inside of the box lid. Store the activities topically, or in an interactive-games box. Box storage can be under tables, or use the boxes as learning-center dividers. If you have an empty closet, cabinets, or shelves you are fortunate.

The hardest objects to store are the large posters and charts. I have found several approaches useful. Cut the posters into three equal sections; tape the sections back together. Apply tape on the back and the front of the chart leaving two clear seams dividing the sections. Fold the charts along the clear seams. This approach makes charts and posters easy to fold and store (please see the drawing below).

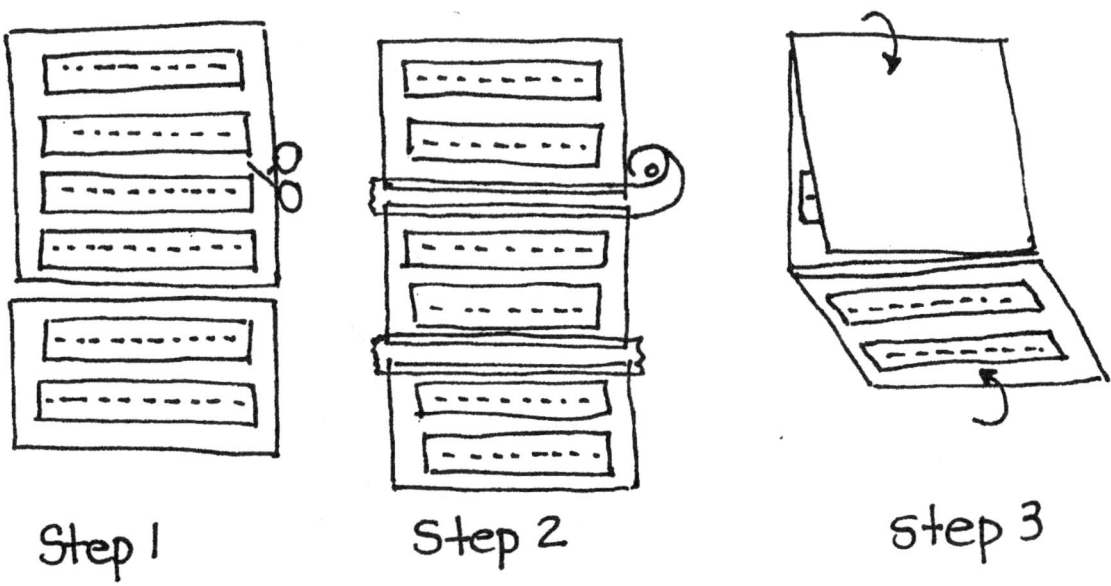

Other suggestions?

- ✓ Purchase commercially made artist's portfolios, or use chart boxes.
- ✓ Use coat hangers on a pocket-chart stand. Attach the charts to the hangers with clothespins.
- ✓ Purchase an over-the-door clothes rack; use coat hangers and pins to hang the charts.
- ✓ A skirt hanger is useful to hang charts. It is flat; the posters can be tiered when attached to the hanger with the clothespins built into the hanger.
- ✓ Have a print shop bind the charts together.
- ✓ Purchase commercially made, large resealable "baggies" (for flat storage).
- ✓ Use two large ceiling hooks (the kind to hang-up bicycles in your garage, for example). Put up the hooks, and punch holes in the top of the charts the same distance as between the hooks; attach notebook rings in the holes and hang charts over the ceiling hooks. To remove a poster, open the ring and remove the poster.

You win the battle of storage by improvising within the space you have. Imagination helps.

If you run across better solutions to the quest for more storage space, be sure to share it with others. Me first! E-mail me at my website, sharon@sharonmacdonald.com .

1. Jingle in My Pocket
By Sharon MacDonald

Five pennies make a nickel.
Two nickels make a dime.
I can trade ten pennies for two nickels or a dime.
Jingle in my pocket, a dollar, and a dime,
A penny and a nickel make me jingle all the time.

Two dimes and a nickel
Make a quarter every time.
I can trade a quarter for three nickels and a dime.
Jingle in my pocket, a dollar, and a dime,
A penny and a nickel make me jingle all the time.

Four quarters make a dollar,
Make a dollar every time.
I can trade four quarters for a dollar any time.
Jingle in my pocket, a dollar, and a dime,
A penny and a nickel make me jingle all the time.

This can be sung to *Mama's Little Baby Likes Shortnin' Bread*.

Activities

1. Make a poster of the poem. Place strips of soft-side Velcro above the money words in the chorus. Copy, color, and cut out the coin pictures below (i.e., penny, nickel, dime, and quarters). Back them with construction paper; laminate them. Put a small piece of hook-side Velcro (or sandpaper) on the back of each coin. The children match the pictures of the coins to the words in the chorus of the poem.

Note: The dollar bill is for teachers to use with older children or children with advanced money skills.

2. Make a large chart like the one on pages 14-15. The chart shows the children how to make change. Copy the pages then color, laminate, and cut out the coins. Give each child a set of paper coins. Have the "make-change" chart visible to all the children in the class. They will use the chart as a guide to make change as they say the poem.

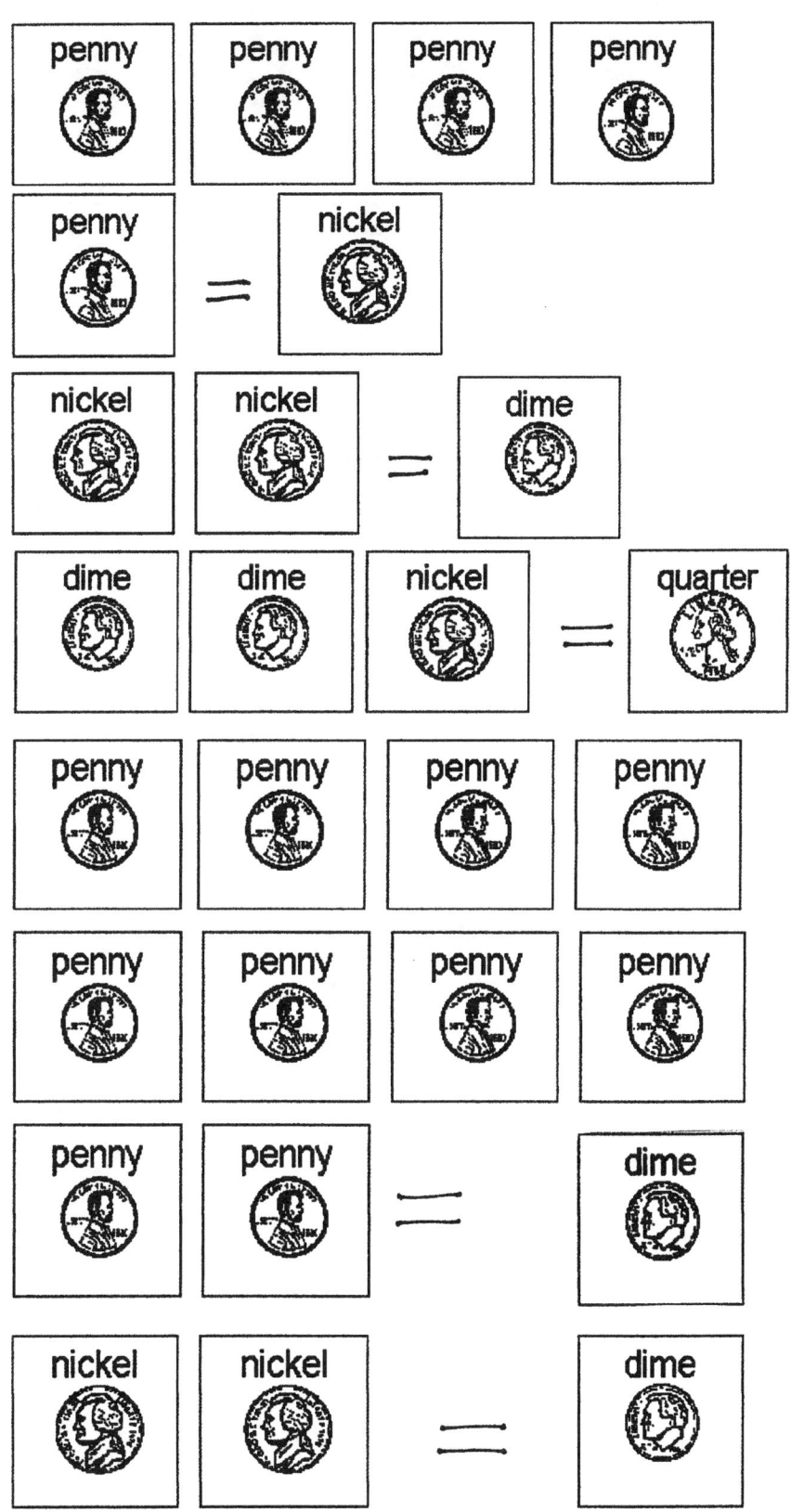

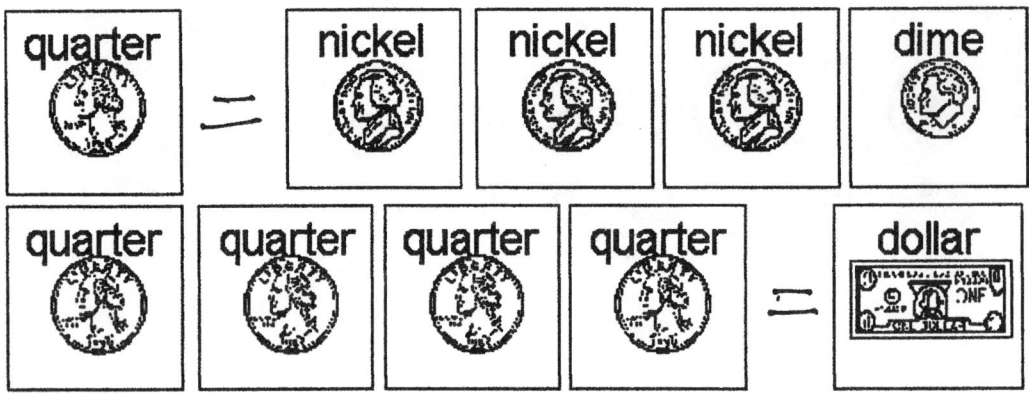

3. Purchase a clear-plastic piggy bank (or use a clear jar with a slit cut in the lid). Put a penny in the piggy bank each day. After five days you will have five pennies; take them out and put in a nickel. Each day, add one more penny. When you have five, take them out and put in another nickel. Then take out the two nickels, put in a dime. The next day add a penny. Add a penny each day until you have five pennies; substitute another nickel. When you have two dimes and five pennies, take out the pennies and replace them with a nickel. Take out all of the coins and put in a quarter. The next day add a penny. Keep this going until you have accumulated $1. The activity can be continued throughout the school year.

Piggy Bank

4. When you say the poem give children several coins to put in their pockets. Have them jingle by shaking the coins in their pockets, by jumping up and down, or by wiggling. If some of the children don't have pockets use a few resealable baggies. Put in the coins and let them jingle.

5. Use Wikki Stiks to outline all the rhyming words in the poem.

6. Write the words to the chorus on sentence strips. In the beginning, cut the sentence strip into four parts, (1) Jingle in my pocket, (2) a dollar and a dime, (3) A penny and a nickel and, (4) Make me jingle all the time. When the children can correctly put together the four parts, cut the strip into individual word segments; have them put together the sentence strips.

7. Have each child select from the poem a coin they would like to be. To help them remember which coin they chose, give them a paper coin. When you recite the chorus of the poem have the children stand up depending on which coin they have chosen to be.

8. Let the children examine a penny carefully; have them look for about a minute. Have them cover the pennies. Have the children tell you what they can remember about the penny. As the children tell you what they saw, make a penny-description chart. Below is a list of many of the characteristics of a penny. After the children have generated their list, and them look at the penny again; add to the list below as necessary.

The Penny

is round
is copper colored
has Lincoln on the face
has the date at the lower right
has the word "Liberty" written on the lower left
has "In God We Trust" written above Lincoln's head
has raised parts
has smooth parts
has a ridge around the edge
has the Lincoln Memorial on the reverse side
has "E Pluribus Unum" written above the Memorial
has "one cent" written below the Memorial
has " United States of America" written above " E Pluribus Unum"
has Lincoln facing to the right

9. Let the children design and then create a grocery store.

(1) Have the children make a newspaper advertisement (show an example from your local newspaper for them to use as a guide).

(2) After looking at a window display or advertisement, have the children design one of their own for display with on-sale products. Cut a square in the side of large cardboard box. Have the children draw their window display on a piece of leftover laminating film. Staple the laminating film on the inside of the opening.

(3) Have the children bring empty food cans from home (Note: ask parents to open the cans at the bottom, rather than the top, and smooth the edges.) They also can bring empty cereal, cookie, and cake boxes to put in their store. Any empty container, safe for children's use, that typically is purchased in a grocery store can be brought to school for inclusion in the children's grocery store. After you put the collection together, have the children price each item by writing the price on an index card and gluing it to the food item.

(4) Collect old, plastic grocery bags and paper grocery sacks for shopping in the store.

(5) For meat items, use rubber toys (i.e., for pets to chew)

(6) Collect plastic fruits and vegetables manufactured for play.

(7) Let the children arrange the items to make shopping easy. Note: This leads to the grouping of similar items, an excellent task to do to teach children to sort by one or more attributes. Have them make large signs to describe the products being sold

(i.e., signs like "DETERGENTS," "CANNED GOODS," "PRODUCE," and "MEAT MARKET".

(8) Make a produce scale using the picture directions below.

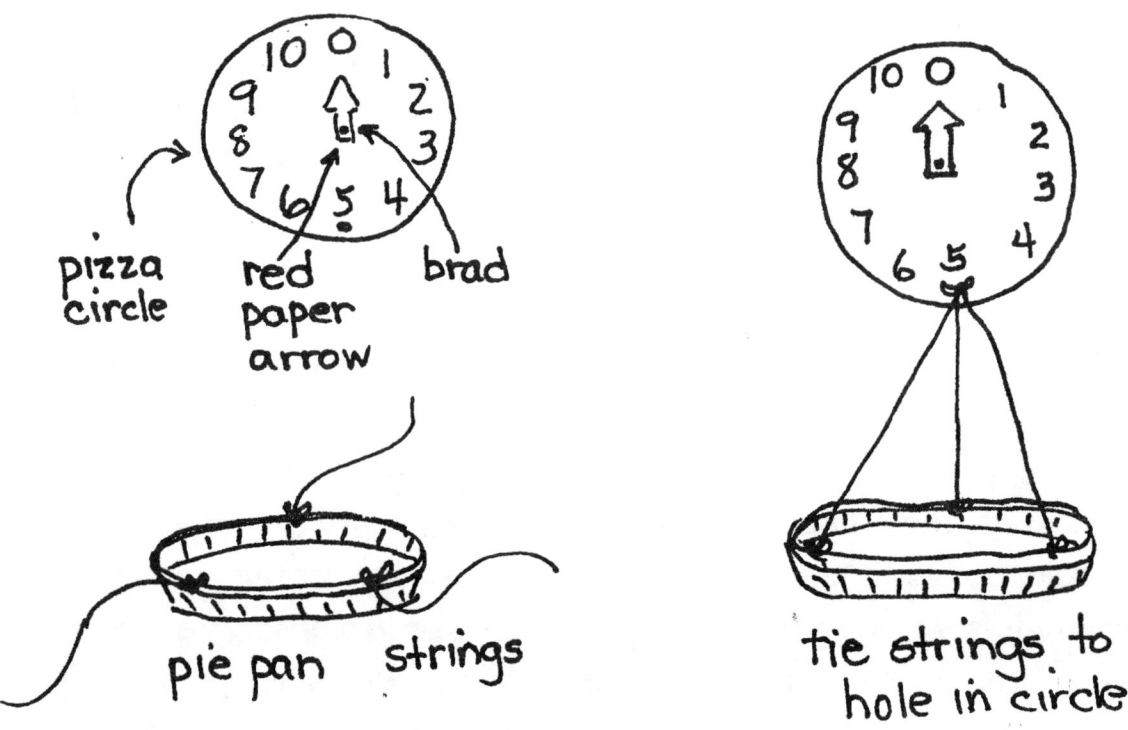

(9) For purchase transactions, use play money or copy the money page in Activity 2 several times; color and cut out the coins.

(10) Have the children design and make a cash register from a cardboard box. Note: they may also want to make a conveyor belt from a cloth, or to make a scanner from a video box with a film canister glued to it.

(11) When the store is ready to do business, open up. Have the children shop, pay, and restock the store.

2. Stack Up the Blocks
By Sharon MacDonald

Stack up the blocks, up so high.
Very tall to touch the sky.
Build a castle, then, a town.
Build them strong so they won't fall down.

Stack up a barn with straight up sides
And curvy roads for tractor rides.
Build a city with signs that show
When to stop and when to go.

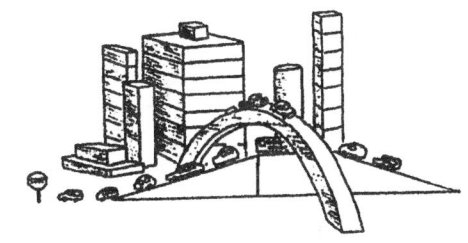

When its time, to end your play
You may hear somebody say,
"Stack up the blocks on the tray
It's time to put them all away."

This can be sung to the tune, *Little Brown Jug*.

Activities

1. Make a poster of the poem.
Copy, color, and cut out the pictures
below. Back them with construction
paper; laminate them. The children
match the pictures to the picture-words
in the poem. To do this, make
a hole above the picture-word
and insert a brad through the
hole from the rear of the poster.
The head of the brad will be resting

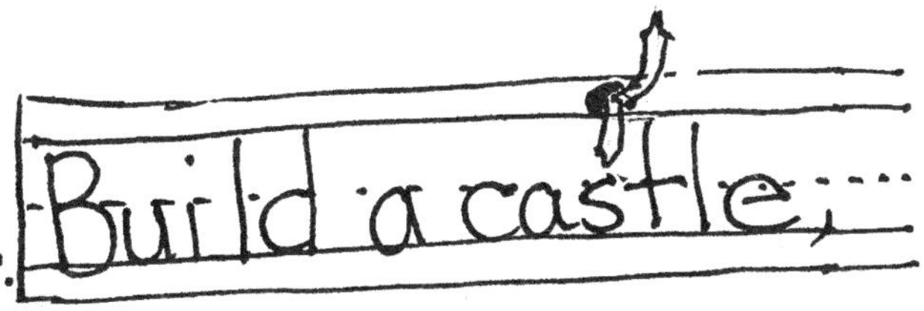

20

on the reverse side of the poster; tape it in place. Fold one of the "legs" of the brad up to make a hook. Fold the other leg against the front of the poster to stabilize the brad.

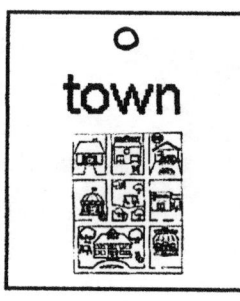

2. Place sheets of drawing paper, crayons, and markers in a basket; the children draw the buildings mentioned in the poem. Put the drawings beside the poem poster.

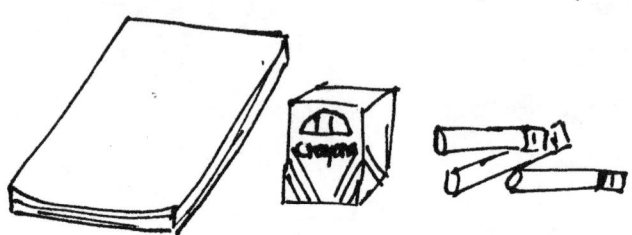

Stack up the blocks, up so high.
Very tall to touch the sky.
Build a castle, then, a town.
Build them strong so they won't fall down.

Stack up a barn with straight up sides
And curvy roads for tractor rides.
Build a city with signs that show
When to stop and when to go.

When its time, to end your play
You may hear somebody say,
"Stack up the blocks on the tray
It's time to put them all away."

3. With tabletop blocks, or in the Block Center, ask the children to build the places talked about in the poem.

4 Find other interesting architectural designs by looking at photographs in a travel magazine. Cut out the interesting ones; display them. Ask the children to build what they see in the photographs.

5. Have the children generate words to replace *castle* or *barn*. Write the words on index cards and put them in a basket beside the poem poster. The children can place the cards over *castle* or *barn* and read the poem with the new word substitution.

6. Use the patterns on page 24 to make street signs. Use *Tinkertoy* sticks and round bases. Copy twice, color, cut out, and glue each sign back-to-back (showing the sign on both sides). Laminate each sign. Put the *Tinkertoy* stick in the base and slip the sign into the slit at the top of the *Tinkertoy* stick. The children use the street signs with their tabletop blocks or in the Block Center.

7. Draw a block structure using large unit block shapes on brown butcher paper; cut it out like the one shown below. Have the children dictate block-building words or words that describe the look and feel of blocks. Write the words on the block-shaped paper; post it in the Block Center. The children add words as they think of them.

8. There is a delightful book titled <u>Architecture Colors,</u> written by M. Crosbie and S. Rosenthal; published by John Wiley and Sons, Inc. It is a book of photographs and paintings of famous structures around the world. It looks at the different colors and elements of these famous constructions.

9. Make paper-bag houses, stores, churches, and schools to use as accessories with the blocks; small paper lunch bags are best. Lay the bag down with folded flap underneath, the back facing up. Have the children draw windows, doors, and decorations on the lunch bags. They can draw on the back, as well, but they will need to hold the folded flap so they can draw under the flap. After they are finished, have them open the bag and sit it upright; the folded flap is the bottom; the "roof" is the open top of the bag.

The children make the stores, churches, and schools in the same way. (You can see samples below.)

Signs for Activity 6

 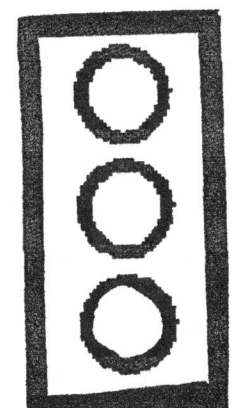 

24

3. <u>What the Animals Said!</u>
By Sharon MacDonald

"Boom, boom!" said the little black cow one day.
"Boom, boom!" said the little black cow.
Think of the shock when he tried to say, "moo"
When "boom" was the moo that he, could do.

"Glug, glug!" said the little pink pig one day.
"Glug, glug!" said the little pink pig.
Think of the shock when he tried to say, "oink"
When "glug" was the oink that he, could do.

"Toot, toot!" said the little yellow chick one day.
"Toot, toot!" said the little yellow chick.
Think of the shock when he tried to say, "peep"
When "toot" was the peep that he, could do.

"Plunk, plunk!" said the little white sheep one day.
"Plunk, plunk!" said the little white sheep.
Think of the shock when he tried to say, "baa"
When "plunk" was the baa that he, could do.

"Hey, Hey!" the farmer said to his brood one day.
"Hey, Hey!" the farmer said to his brood.
Think of the shock when his animals said
"Plunk, plunk, toot, toot, glug, glug, boom, boom!"

Activities

1. Make a poster of the poem. Copy, color and cut out the farm animal pictures below. Back them with construction paper; laminate them. On the right side of the poster beside each verse, place a strip of soft-side Velcro. Put small pieces of hook-side Velcro on the back of the animal pictures. Have the children match the picture of the animal to the correct verse.

"Boom, boom!" said the little black cow one day.

"Boom, boom!" said the little black cow.

Think of the shock when he tried to say, "moo"

When "boom" was the moo that he, could do.

2. Place a basket of index cards and pencils below the poster. Have the children write silly animal sounds to replace the ones in the poem.

To make the activity more challenging: place a folder of drawing paper, and a basket of markers and crayons, under the poem poster.

Have the children draw other farm animals making unusual sounds; have them use a "speech bubble" to show each animal's unusual sound.

3. Cut a 2" x 2" square of each of the following colors from construction paper: yellow, black, white, and pink. Write the color word on each square. Laminate the squares and place a small piece of hook-side Velcro on the back of the square. Have the children match the square to the verse with the appropriate color word in it. (Note: the squares will stick to the piece of soft-side Velcro that you put on the poem poster for Activity 1.)

4. Make a poem book illustrated with the children's drawings. Focus on keywords. Keywords are words you want the children to learn to read, to say, and to recognize.

Step 1. Collect 12 sheets of 18" x 24" construction paper, 23 sentence strips, 3 notebook rings, markers and crayons.

Step 2. Write one line of the poem on each sentence strip.

"Boom, boom!" said the little black cow one day.

Step 3. Glue two lines of the poem along the 24" bottom of the construction paper.

Step 4. There will be 10 pages in the poem book for the children to work on. Have the children work in pairs to draw an illustration above the part of the poem that you have glued to the bottom of the page. Have a pair of children make a book cover; have them write the title and illustrate the cover. If the children do not write yet, use a sentence strip; write the title on the strip and glue it in the center of the cover.

Step 5. After the children have contributed their illustrations, laminate the pages and the cover. Put the book together with the three notebook rings.

Step 6. To make the book interactive, use the last two sentence strips to write the words "Boom, boom," "moo," or "black cow" (from the first verse); "Glug, glug," "oink, or "pink pig" (from the second verse); "Toot, toot," "peep," or "yellow chick" (from the third verse); "Plunk, plunk," "baa," or "white sheep," (from the fourth verse); and "Hey, hey," or "farmer" (from the last verse). Cut the words from the sentence strip and laminate them.

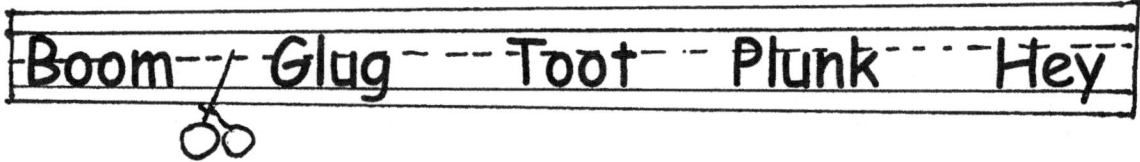

Step 7. On the first two lines of each of the verses, make a pocket-over-the-word by cutting a strip of leftover laminating film to fit the words on the sentence strips in the book. Use clear-plastic tape to attach the film over the words. Be sure to attach the tape along the bottom and along each side of the laminating film only. <u>Do not put tape across the top of the laminating film</u> (please see below).

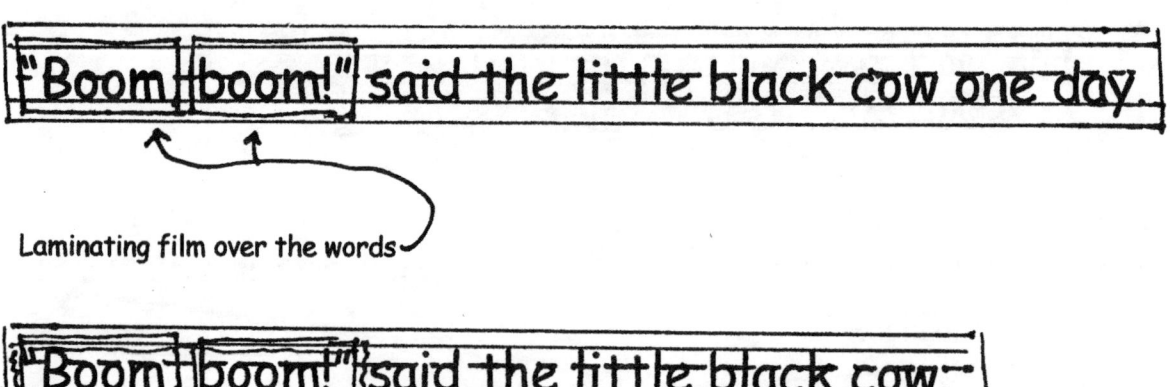

29

Step 8. Place the words in a large resealable baggie and put the baggie with the book. When the children read the book they match the words to the correct word in the book.

To make this more challenging, write the verses on sentence strips but leave out the keywords. Write the keywords on a separate sentence strip; cut the keywords apart. Have the children fill in the missing keyword just as you would if they were matching the keywords with the pictures. In this instance, however, you are asking the child to find the word that belongs in the blank space.

5. Mike Artell has a wonderful book about farm animals and the sounds they make. It is entitled Who Said "Moo"? published by Macmillian, 1994. It is easy for the children to read along.

6. The children can add new verses by changing the farm animal or the unusual word it says in the song; or, by changing the actual sound that the farm animal makes. You can do this activity also with zoo animals, circus animals, and pets.

7. If you have puppets of the animals in the poem, let the children use them as they say the poem.

8. If it is possible, visit a farm so the children can see and hear the animals and the sounds they make.

9. Have the children identify the "oo" sound in "boom," "moo," and "toot." Have them find the "double e" in "peep" and "sheep." Have them identify the ending "g" sound in "pig" and "glug."

4. What Can You Do?
By Sharon MacDonald

Here is my head, what can it do?
It can nod, nod at you.
Nod, nod, that's what it can do!

Here are eyes, what can they do?
They can wink, wink at you.
Wink, wink, that's what they can do!

Here are my ears, what can they do?
They can listen, listen to you.
Listen, listen, that's what they can do!

Here are my arms, what can they do?
They can wave, wave at you.
Wave, wave, that's what they can do!

Here are my hands, what can they do?
They can clap, clap with you.
Clap, clap, that's what they can do!

Here are my legs, what can they do?
They can hop, hop to you.
Hop, hop, that's what they can do!

Here are my feet, what can they do?
They can tip toe, tip toe to you.
Tip toe, tip toe, that's what they can do!

Activities

1. Make a poem poster. Copy, color, and cut out the pictures below; back them with construction paper and laminate them. Put a small piece of magnetic tape on the back of each picture. Place a small piece of magnetic tape on the right side of the poster beside each verse. The children will match each body part to the verse in which the body part is said (please see below).

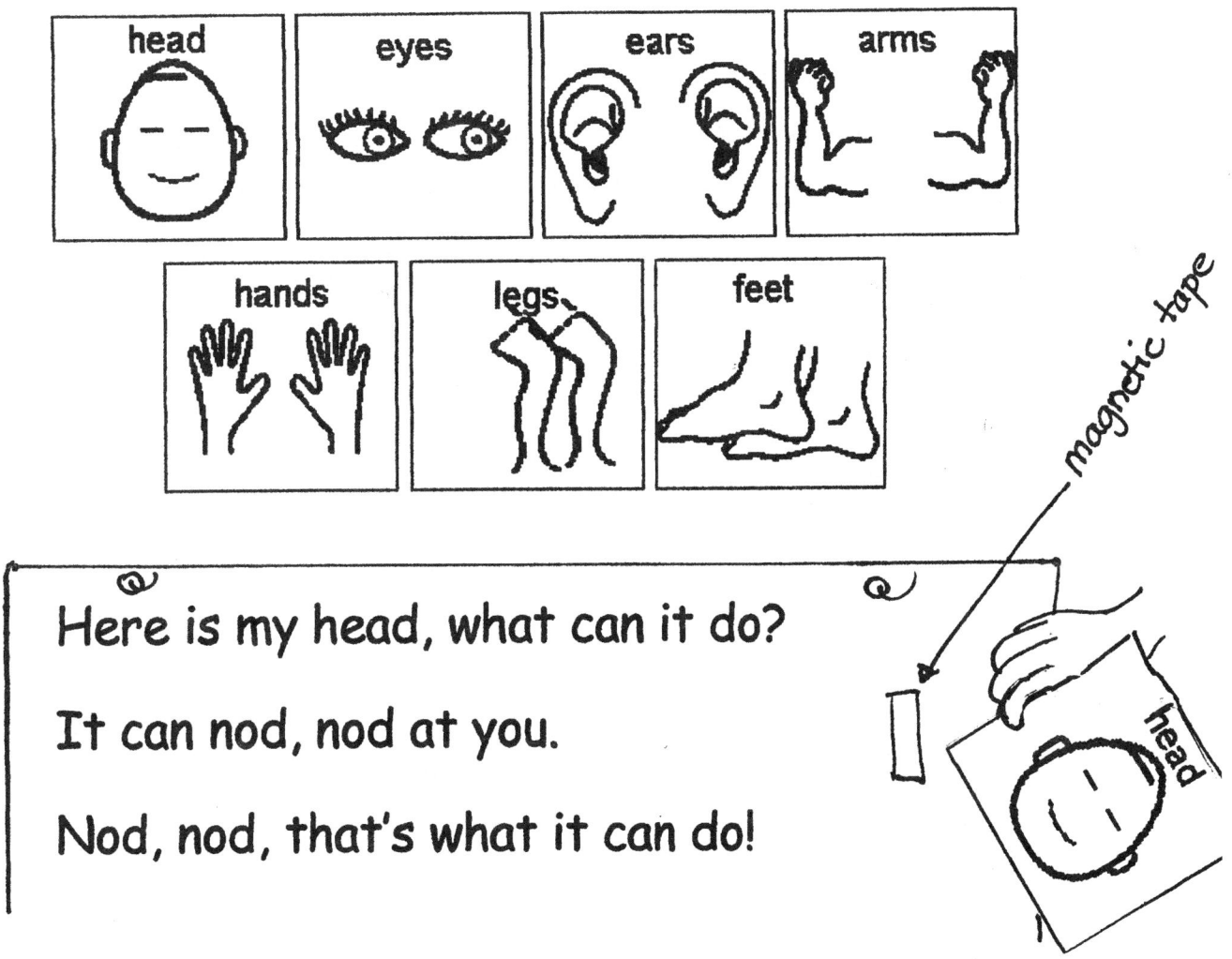

Here is my head, what can it do?

It can nod, nod at you.

Nod, nod, that's what it can do!

After the children have successfully matched the pictures to the body parts, write index cards with just the words on them. Have the children match the index-card words to the words on the poem chart.

2. Act out the movements in the poem using each body part.

3. Have the children make up new verses to the poem using other body parts; use movements like the elbow-flap and the knee-bend. If they have developed writing skills, have sentence strips available for them to write their own verses.

4. For very young children, use a doll to show the body parts; have them use the doll to do the movements.

5. For the older children, work on identifying the two-vowels-side-by-side rule in the words "head," "toe," and "feet"; the short vowel sounds in the words "nod," "wink," "legs," "clap," "hop," and "tip"; and, the long-vowel-silent-ending-"e" rule in "wave." Have them use highlighter tape over the words or *Wikki Stiks* around the words.

6. To make it more challenging for older children, work on punctuation like the question mark (?) and the exclamation mark (!). When the children say the poem, for example, they can shrug their shoulders when they see a question mark and hold one hand in the air when they see an exclamation point.

7. Have the children put together a child's-body puzzle. Use the drawing on Page 34. Copy it twice. Use the first copy as a puzzle base; cut the second copy into as many puzzle pieces as your children can work successfully. Put it out for the children to work. Note: the puzzle base helps the children solve the puzzle. If the children need more help, trace the puzzle pieces on the puzzle base so the children can use the silhouettes of the pieces to guide them to a solution.

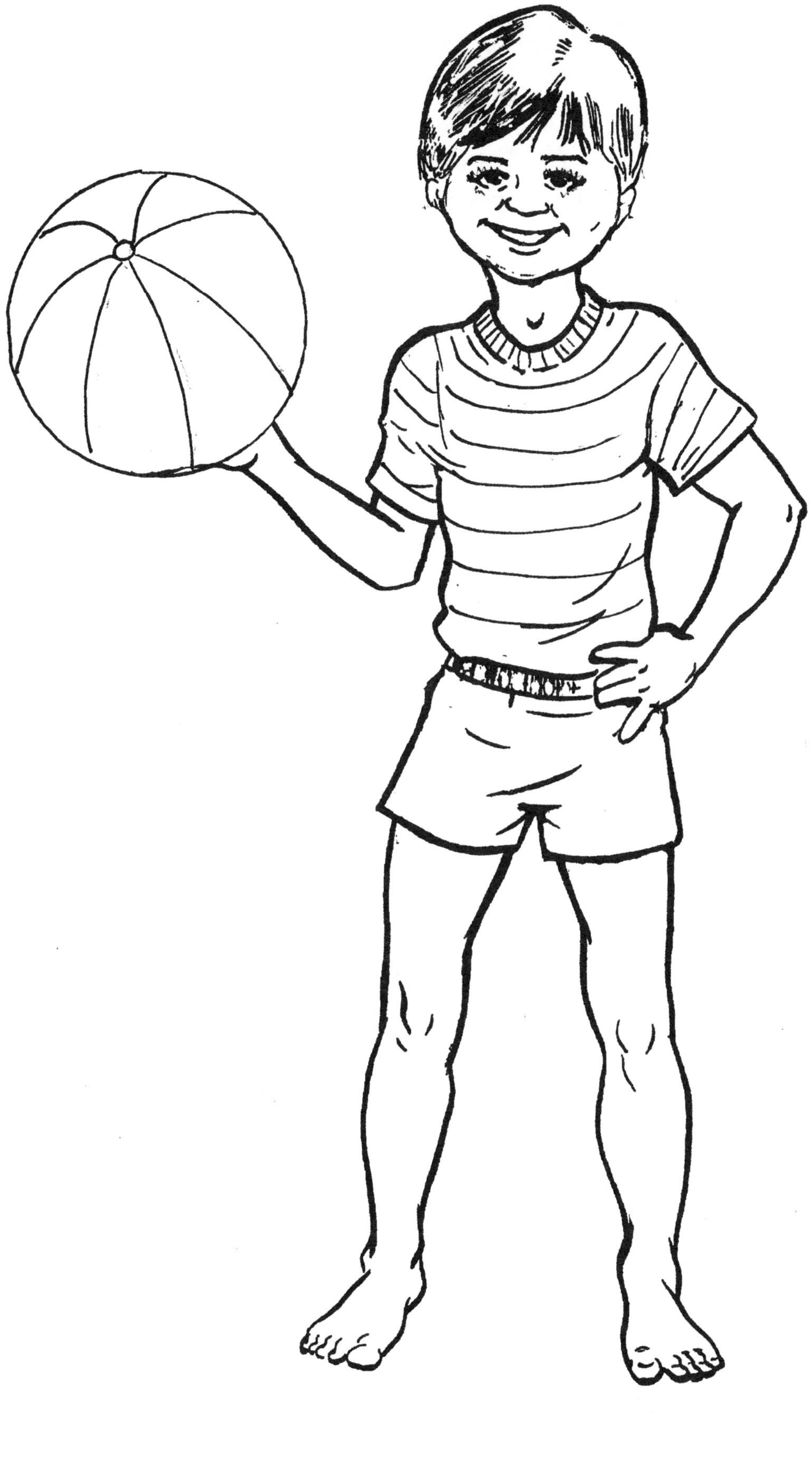

5. Multi-plenti-cation
By Sharon MacDonald

Multi-plenti-cation
Is how crayon boxes grow.
It's a name that I can say
And, it's the biggest word I know.
A box of sixteen crayons
Is two times a box of eight.

'Round, and 'round, they go!

A box of brand-new crayons
Were made for kids, you know.
The ends are nice and pointy
They can scribble fast or slow.
The crayons stand right up
In a neatly colored row.

'Round, and 'round, they go.

There are several colors
That we like to choose.
We like the reds, the greens,
The yellows and the blues.
I share them with my friends
And they share theirs with me.

'Round and 'round they go!

Activities

1. Have crayon boxes containing 8, 16, 24, 48, 64 crayons. Let the children compare the size boxes and the number of crayons and colors in each box.

2. Have the children graph the crayons in a box 16, 24, or 48 crayons (chose the size box that best meets the developmental level of your children). On the graph, write "RED," "YELLOW," "BLUE" and "DOES NOT BELONG" in four boxes along the bottom. The children will sort the crayons into the four categories. Let them negotiate which crayon color would best be sorted into the four categories and why (please see drawing below).

Red	Yellow	Blue	Does not Belong

3. Read the poem into a tape recorder. Copy the poem, back it with construction paper and laminate it. Provide drawing paper and a box of 8 crayons. Put the tape, the poem, drawing paper, and the crayons in a large resealable baggie; put it in the Library

Center next to the tape recorder. The children put in the tape and listen or draw along as the tape plays.

4. Make a poem poster and laminate it. Use highlighter tape to mark the crayon words, the color words; the "t"s, "sh"s and the "ch"; and highlight all the " 'round" words. Choose the words and word parts that are suitable for your children.

5. Place a basket of magnet letters and a small magnet board beneath the poem poster. Have the children spell some of the words they "read" in the poem using the magnet letters.

6. Make a three-dimensional puzzle by cutting apart a crayon box; have the children put it together using the picture directions below.

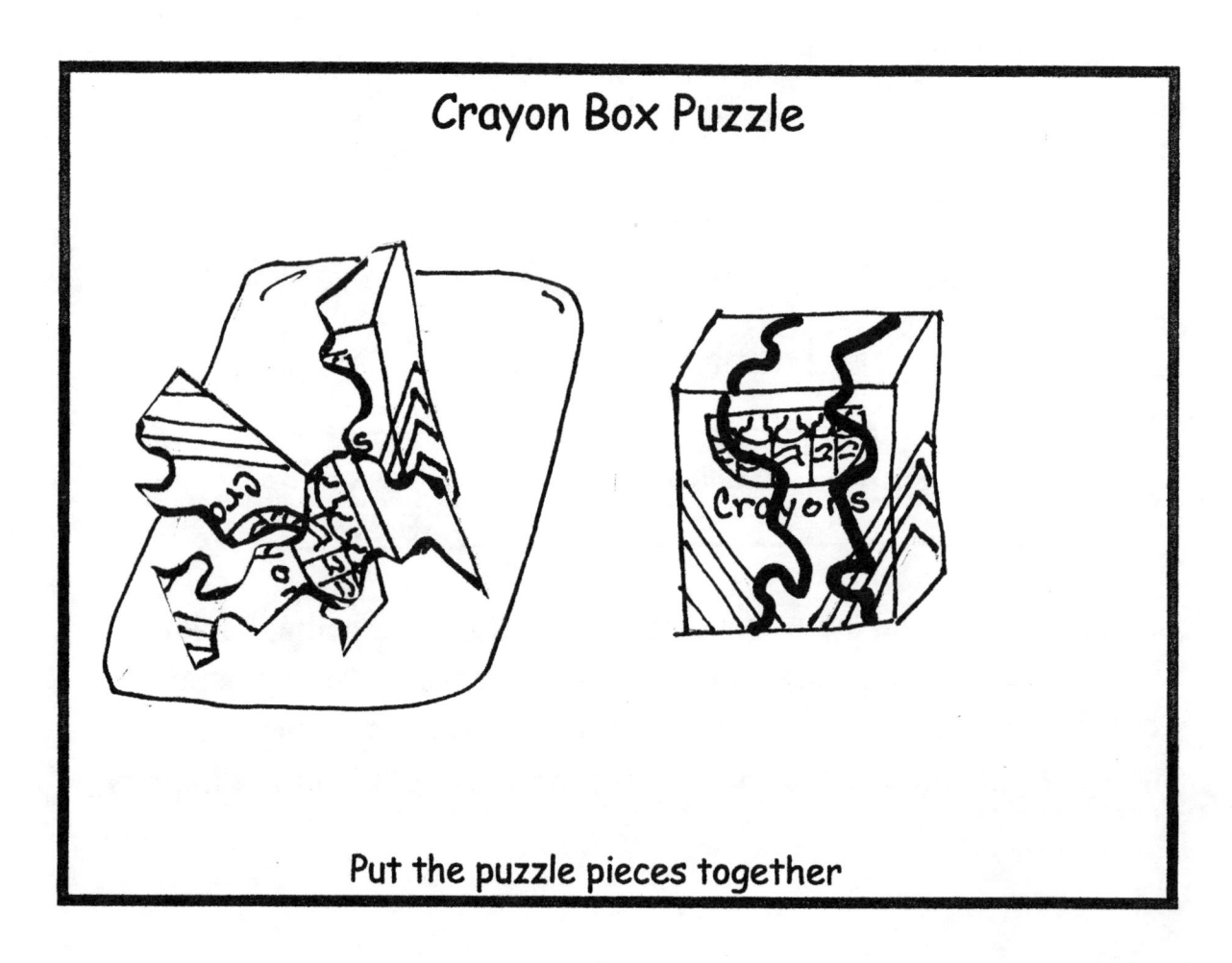

Crayon Box Puzzle

Put the puzzle pieces together

7. Collect 12 crayons of various colors. On a sheet of 8 ½ x 11 paper, color 12 areas about one-inch square with each of the crayons. Have the children match the crayons to its color. Make this activity more or less challenging by increasing or decreasing the number of crayon-color choices. If you use a box of multicolored-crayons with various shades of brown that must be matched you are making the activity more challenging. If you use just primary and secondary colors the activity is less challenging.

8. Collect jumbo-, large-, and regular size crayons (sometimes you can find small crayons to add this activity). Have the children seriate them by crayon circumference.

9. Write the following words on a sentence strip: "'round and 'round they go." Cut them into individual words. Have the children use a pocket chart to put the words together as they occur in the poem. To extend the activity difficulty, have them arrange them in any order and then read what they have said. For example: *"Go they round and round";* or *"Round go they and round."*

10. Give the children each a piece of sandpaper and a crayon. Have them draw on the sandpaper "'round and 'round," like the words in the poem. Encourage them to press hard when coloring

38

on the sandpaper. Ask them to color on a sheet of regular paper. Compare and discuss the differences in the surfaces.

11. Make a number-matching board, like the one below. Here's how. Glue one through 10 crayons to individual, 4" x 6" cards made from heavy cardboard. For example, put one crayon on the first card, two crayons on the second, three on the third, and so on, up to 10. Cover an old game board with white contact paper. Draw 10, 4" x 6" rectangles on the game board for each of the numbers "1" through "10." Write the word "one" across the top of the first rectangle; write the number "1" at the bottom of the first rectangle. Write "two" and "2" on the second rectangle, write "three" and "3" on the third, and so on, through the tenth card. The children match their cards to the correct numbers on the board.

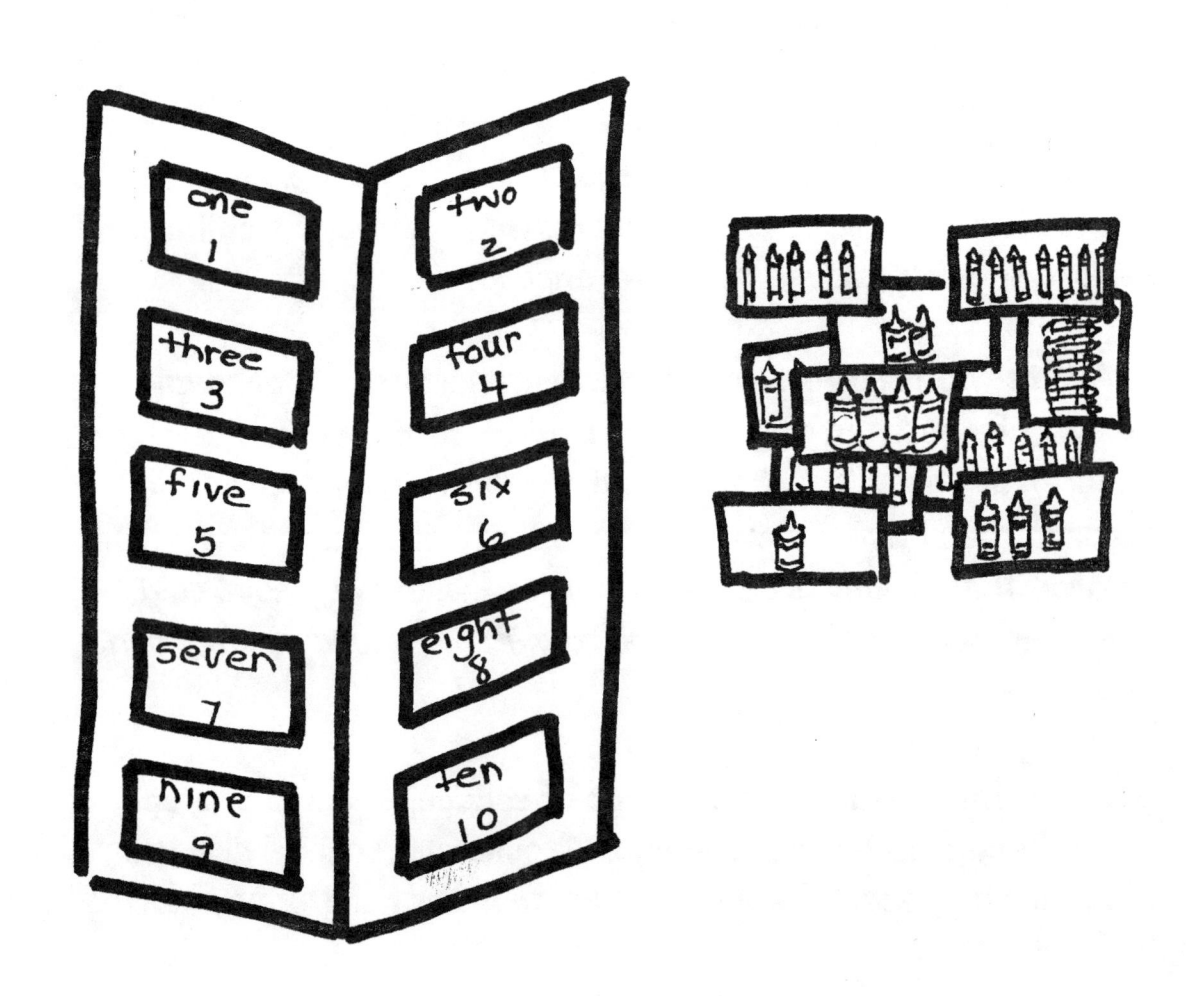

6. Fuzzy Caterpillar
By Sharon MacDonald

A fuzzy caterpillar
Appeared upon my shoe
And yelled to me quite clearly,
"I don't believe it's true."

The fuzzy caterpillar
Crawled up my blue-jean pants
He curled his brow and said,
"It doesn't happen to ants."

I said to him, "What happens?"
He cocked his head and cried,
"Not too long from now,
I'll be butterflied."

Caterpillar-butterflied today...
Gonna flap his wings and fly away.
I'd like to see him make a start today
Caterpillar-butterflied that way.

Caterpillar-butterflied today...
Gonna flap his wings and fly away,
In the bushes and the flowers he'll play.
Caterpillar-butterflied

Then, the fuzzy caterpillar
Ooched right up my shirt.
And said a little sadly,
"I hope it doesn't hurt."

"I hope so too," I said,
"You don't have to cry
I think its kind of neat
When caterpillars fly."

Well, that's the last I saw of him.
He perked up then crawled away.
He wanted to be alone I guess
To butterfly that day.

Caterpillar-butterflied today...
Gonna flap his wings and fly away,
In the bushes and the flowers he'll play.
Caterpillar-butterflied.

Activities

1. Have the children re-tell and dramatize the story of the caterpillar in the poem.

2. With older children, have them illustrate and write their own caterpillar story. Have them make blank books, like the one shown below, to write and to illustrate their story. Encourage them to use their own style. Ask them to use speech bubbles when the child and the caterpillar talk.

Here are the instructions to make a six-page writing book:

(1) Fold two 8-½" x 11" sheets of paper into a hamburger.

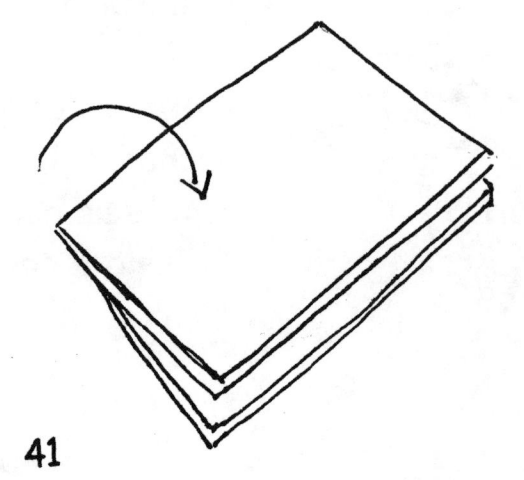

(2) With the two sheets folded together, cut two, 1-¼" slits from the edges of both sheets, toward the center.

(3) Fold a third sheet of paper into a hamburger. Measure and mark one inch from both sides, along the fold. Cut a thin section with scissors starting from the first mark, continuing to the second. When completed, you will have a long, thin window in which to insert the two sheets of paper from Instruction (1). and (2). above.

(4) Roll the two sheets together and slide them into the window in the middle of the third sheet [see Instruction (3). above]. Release the rolled pages.
You will have made a six-page book for the children to write their stories.

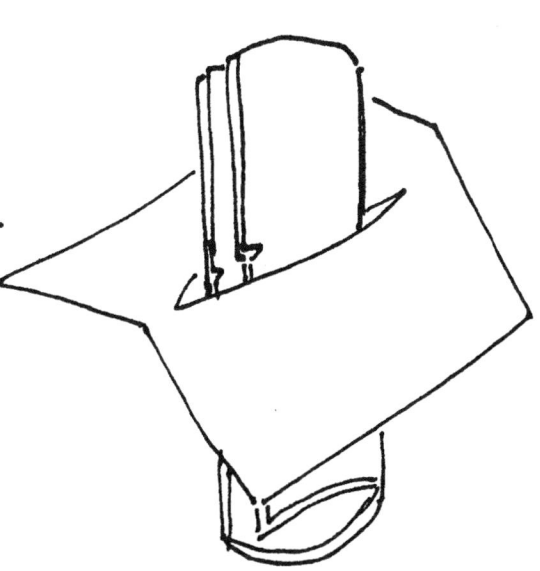

3. Write the first three verses on a chart; omit the last word in each verse; but leave a space for the word. Make a hole above the word-space and attach a brad through the back of the chart; the "legs" will stick out through the front. Tape the head to the back surface of the chart. Fold the legs in the shape of a hook. Copy the words that go in the word-spaces in each verse, laminate them; make a hole in the top with a hole-punch. Have the children say the first three verses and find the missing word in each verse. Put up the word card on the brad-hook when the children select the word that goes in that space. Repeat the activity for the last three verses.

A fuzzy caterpillar

Appeared upon my shoe

And yelled to me quite clearly,

"I don't believe it's _____." [true]

The fuzzy caterpillar

Crawled up my blue-jean pants

He curled his brow and said,

"It doesn't happen to _____."

I said to him, "What happens?"

He cocked his head and cried,

"Not too long from now,

I'll be _____."

[Butterflied] [ants]

4. Copy the blank music sheet on page 47; encourage the children to write their own story-poems and write (i.e., pretend to write) music for it.

5. Teach the children the American Sign Language for "Butterfly." Please see the illustration below.

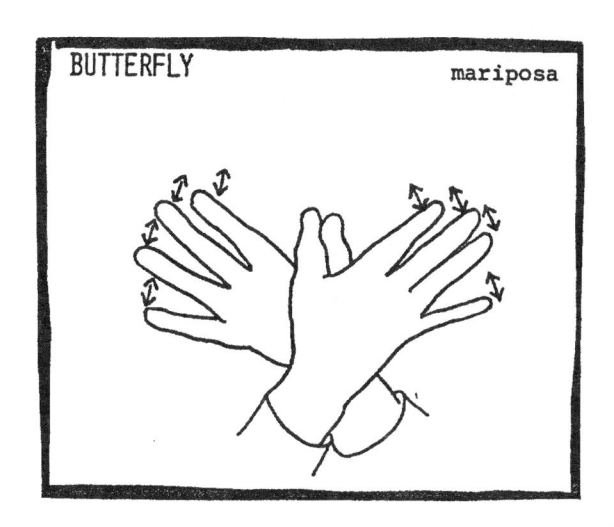

6. Use the card below to make a set of butterfly-life-cycle sequence cards. Copy, color and cut out the cards. Back them with construction paper and laminate them. Follow the directions on page 45 to make a lunch-bag sequence board. The children store the pieces inside the lunch bag; when they take them out, they sequence the cards on the lunch-bag board.

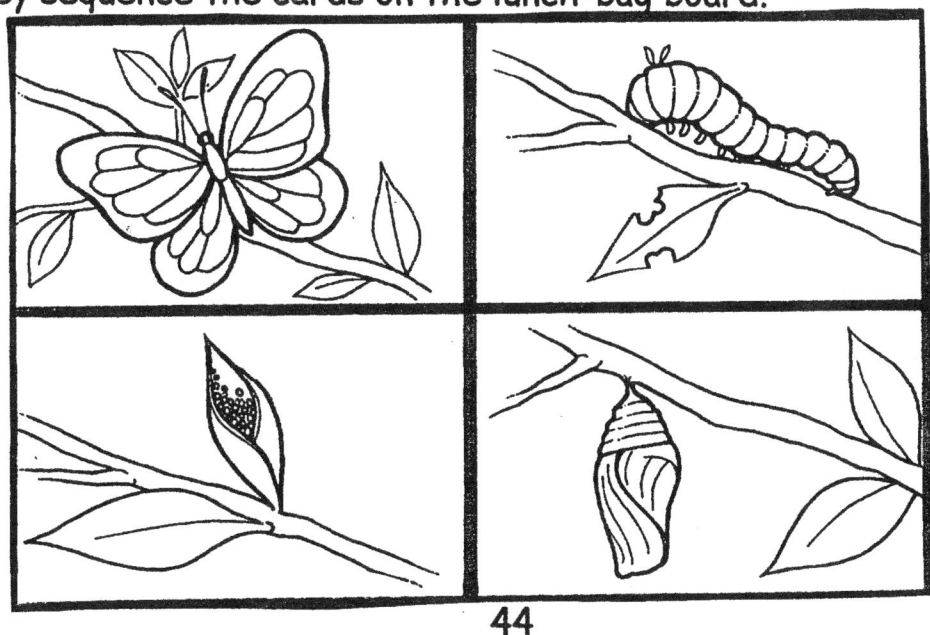

The Life Cycle of a Butterfly

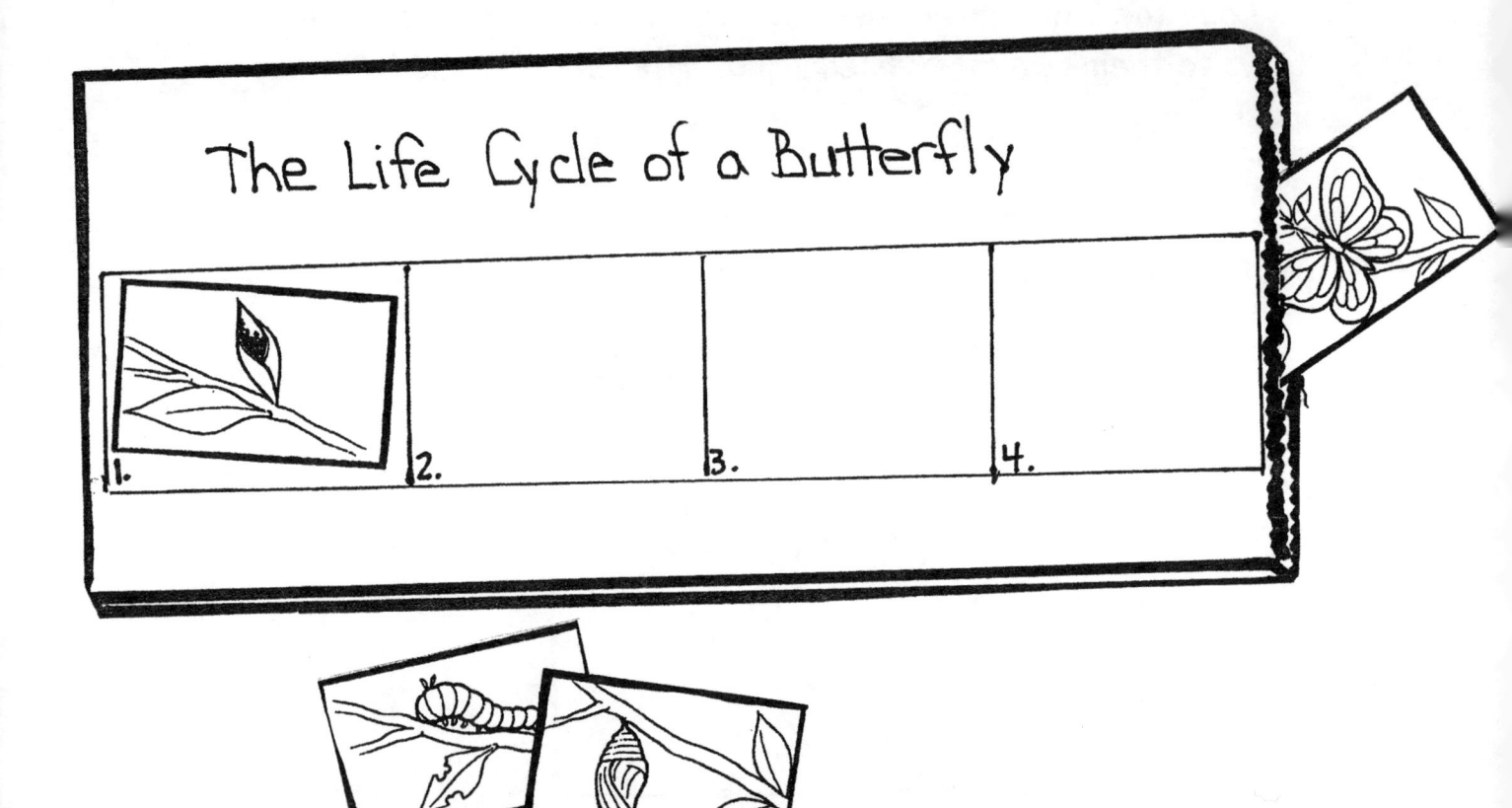

7. An alternative to doing life-cycle cards is making life-cycle bracelets. Collect large, cardboard packing-tape cylinders. Glue each life cycle stage picture on a cylinder. (Note: if the pictures are too large, reduce them to fit the cylinders.) Have the children put on their butterfly bracelets, one at a time, in life-development order.

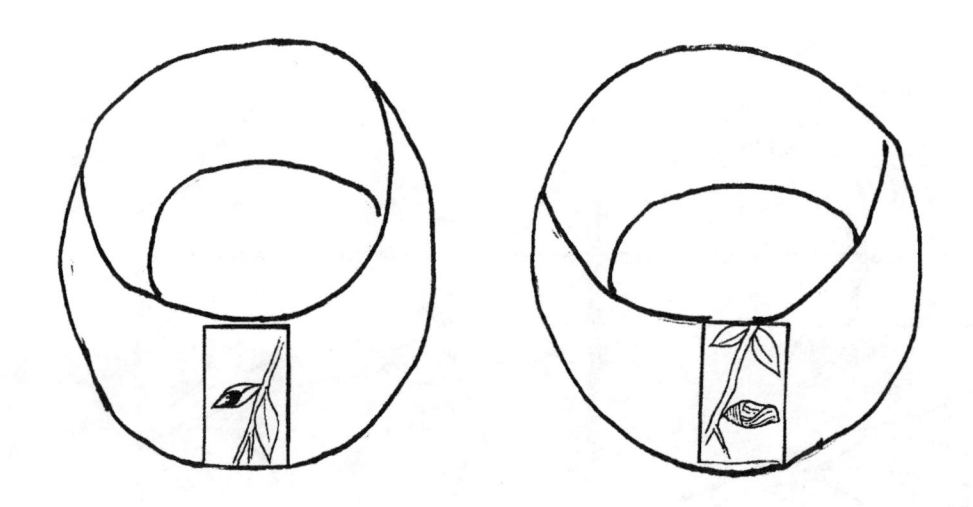

8. There are many skills that can be learned by taking one verse of the poem and putting it on a large chart. It is called a poem chart. I have used them often. During group time you can use the following ideas for activities:

spacing between words • syllables

capital letters → A fuzzy caterpillar

Appeared upon my shoe

And yelled to me quite clearly, ← suffixes

contractions "I don't believe it's true."

punctuation • rhyming words

9. Find a large picture of a butterfly. Copy it five times making each copy smaller so you have six different sizes of butterflies for the children to seriate by size.

10. Find a large picture of a butterfly and cut it into puzzle pieces for the children to work.

11. Purchase a butterfly kit and hatch butterflies. Keep a journal of the changes that occur during the cycle. Keep a time line to track how many days for the complete life cycle to evolve and to see how many days between each change. Take photographs of each stage in the cycle and then have the children put them in order.

Music Sheet

47

7. Five Round Pumpkins
By Sharon MacDonald

Five round pumpkins in a roadside store
One became a jack-o-lantern; then there were four.
Four round pumpkins as orange as can be
One became a pumpkin pie; then there were three.

Three round pumpkins with nothing fun to do
One was cooked as pumpkin bread; then there were two.
Two round pumpkins sitting in the sun
One was cooked as pancakes; then there was one

One round pumpkin, one job was left undone
He was kept to make new seeds; then there were none.
One round pumpkin, one job was left undone
He was kept to make new seeds; then there were none.

This can be sung to *Five Little Honeybuns*.

Activities

1. Make a poster of the poem. Place two strips of soft-side *Velcro* along the sides of the poem, from the top of the poem to the bottom. Put the first strip down the left side of the poem, the second along the right side.

Copy, color, back with construction paper, cut out, and laminate the pictures *and* the numbers on page 49. Place a small piece of hook-side *Velcro* on the back of each picture and each number. To do the activity the children will match each picture to the number word by placing the picture next to the line in the poem that has the word. For the pictures use the right side. For the numbers, use the left side. The children will match to the numbers using the *Velcro* strip along the left side of the poem.

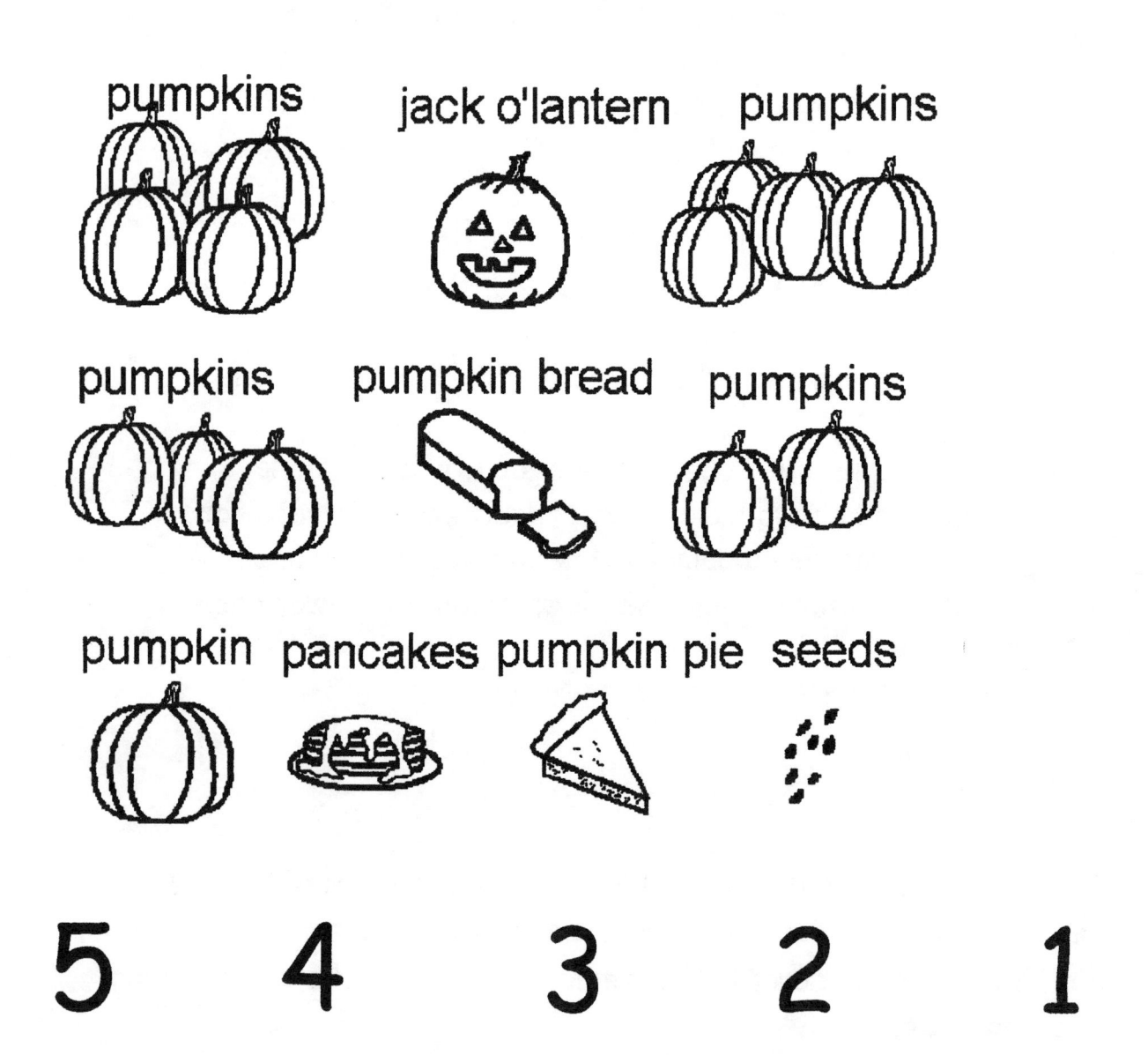

pumpkins   jack o'lantern   pumpkins

pumpkins   pumpkin bread   pumpkins

pumpkin   pancakes   pumpkin pie   seeds

5   4   3   2   1

2. Have a pumpkin seed cook-off

You'll need a cup or two of raw pumpkin seeds (enough for each child to have a snack) and vegetable oil, a cookie sheet, a tablespoon, a measuring cup, a large bowl, a long-handled stirring spoon, and paper serving cups. Mix in a bowl one cup of pumpkin seeds with 1-tablespoon of vegetable oil. Have each child that wants to stir use the spoon to move the seeds around in the oil. Pour the oil-coated seeds onto the baking tray; spread them out. Preheat the oven to 350 degrees. Cook for 10-12 minutes. The seeds are done when they are crisp and slightly browned. Sprinkle the seeds with a little salt. When they have cooled, serve them up in the paper cups for the children's snack.

To make this activity more challenging: cook the seeds using the recipe above; then, cook up another batch in an electric skillet. Have the children make comparisons, state their preferences, and graph the results. To make it simpler: take a few children at a time to observe the seeds as they are cooking. [Note: it is hard for younger children to remember what the seeds looked like **before** they were cooked, so let them see the changes frequently. They will grasp the concept of change by seeing increments of change often. Young children must observe many times to get the gist of it. It is helpful to keep several raw pumpkin seeds around, just for comparison.]

| Mix 1 cup of pumpkin seeds and 1 tablespoon of oil. | Spread the seeds on a tray. | Bake at 350 for 10 minutes. | Sprinkle with salt. Eat! |

3. Make pumpkin pancakes.

To make pumpkin pancakes you will need these ingredients and utensils:

pancake mix	measuring cup	large bowl
2 eggs	teaspoon	honey or syrup
ground cinnamon	stirring spoon	paper plates
canned pumpkin	spatula	napkins
margarine	electric skillet	forks

Mix 4-cups pancake mix and 1 teaspoon of cinnamon. Add 2 eggs and 1 cup of pumpkin meat. Stir well. Preheat the electric skillet to 350 degrees. Add a slice of margarine. After it melts, pour four-inch circles of batter in the skillet. Cook until bubbles form on the top of the pancakes; flip them with the spatula and cook until golden brown. Serve with margarine and syrup, or honey (please see the drawings below).

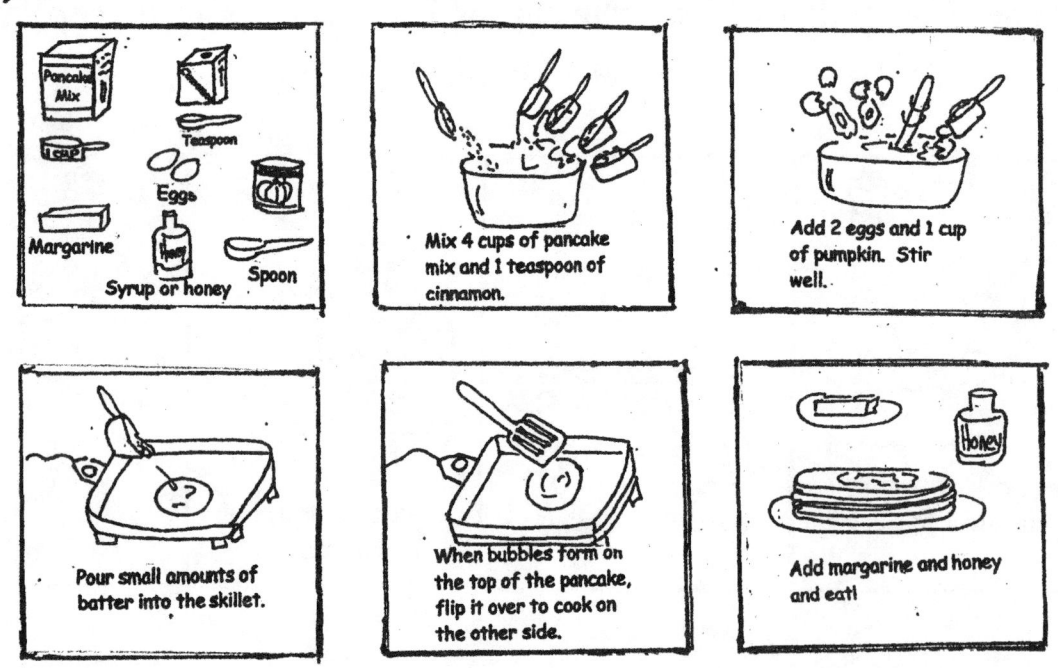

4. As a follow up to making pumpkin pancakes, read Tomie DePaola's book, <u>Pancakes for Breakfast</u>, or Eric Carle's book, <u>Pancakes, Pancakes</u>.

5. Make a pumpkin pie.

You will need:

baked pie shell	cloves	1 cup measuring cup
canned pumpkin	ginger	½ cup measuring cup
brown sugar	vanilla	1 tablespoon
white sugar	dark corn syrup	1 teaspoon
cinnamon	eggs	½ teaspoon
salt	double boiler	1/8 teaspoon
evaporated milk	whisk	mixing bowl

Mix in a double boiler 1-½ cup, canned pumpkin; 1-½ cup, evaporated milk; 6-tablespoons brown sugar; 2-tablespoons, white sugar; and ½-teaspoon, salt. To this mixture add 1/8-teaspoon, cloves; 1-teaspoon, cinnamon, ½-teaspoon, ginger, and ½-cup, dark corn syrup. Stir well. Break 3 eggs in a bowl. Beat them gently. Put the double boiler on medium heat. Pour the beaten eggs into the mixture in the double boiler and stir well. Cook this until it is thick; remove from the heat. Add 1-teaspoon, vanilla. Pour this hot mixture into the baked pie shell and cool. When it is cool, it is time to eat the pie.

6. Make a pumpkin seed puff book. Fold, open, cut, re-fold, and puff into a book the poem sheet is on page 54. Here's how:

1. Fold an 8-1/2' x 11" piece of paper like a hamburger (please see below).

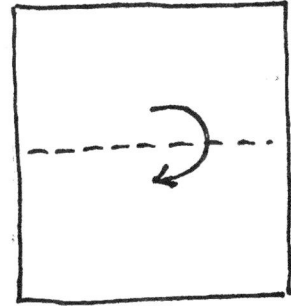

2. Fold it again like a hot dog.

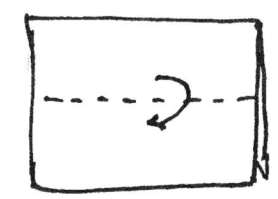

3. Fold it again into a burrito.

4. Unfold the burrito-fold, then, unfold the hot dog fold, to the point shown in # 1 above. With the folded side up, cut in the middle of the sheet from the first fold to the second.

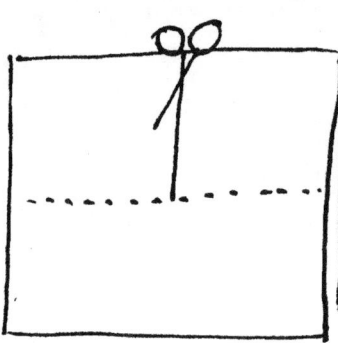

5. Unfold the entire page.

6. Fold into a hot dog with the cut on the fold.

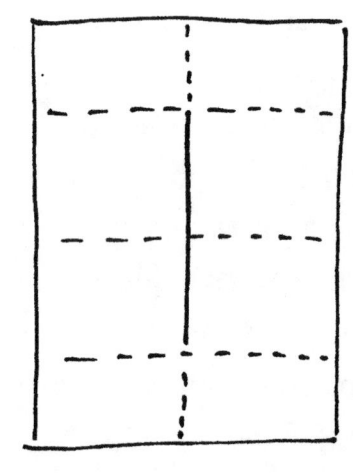

7. Puff out the book center by pushing inward on both ends, forcing the center outward, as shown below.

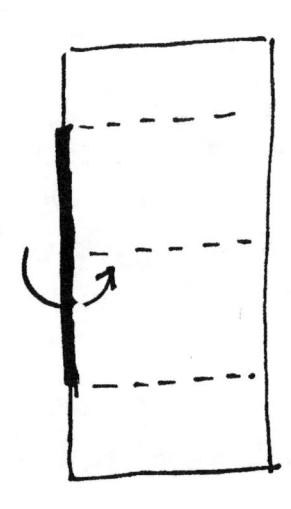

8. Fold the pages together. Read your book!

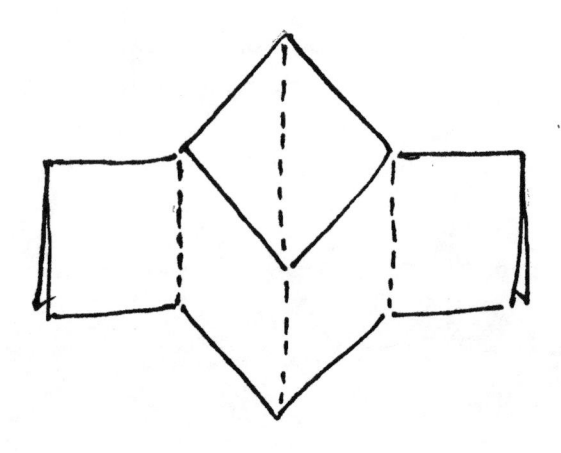

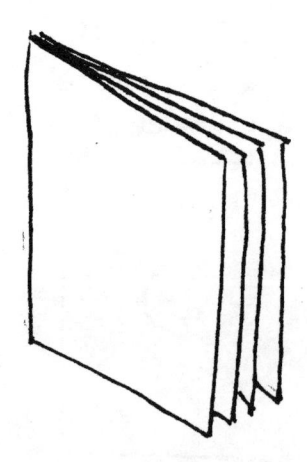

53

The Pumpkin Seed
By Sharon MacDonald

The package said pumpkin seeds.
I know it's true
'cause I can read.

I put the seeds into the ground
and watered carefully all around.

Soon, the seeds sprouted and started to grow.
But how it knew to, I'll never know.

The vine grew outward very low.
Up, wasn't the way it wanted to go.
Flowers blossomed—
some here, some there.
And small orange balls were Everywhere.

As fall slowly ceased to be,
the orange balls smiled pumpkin at me.

I understand that pumpkin smile,
'cause each one of them knew all the while...

---

that in each seed hidden secretly,
is pumpkin knowledge of what to be.

7. The "flip book" partially drawn below consists of six panels that can be "read" along with the *Five Round Pumpkins* poem. The child, to reveal what the pumpkin becomes, can lift each panel in succession, as he reads the poem. For example, the first pumpkin is used to "make a jack-o'-lantern." When the first panel is raised, a jack-o'-lantern is revealed and four pumpkins remain. The second pumpkin is used "to make pumpkin pie." When the second panel is raised, a pumpkin pie is revealed and three pumpkins remain, and so on, to end of the poem when the fifth pumpkin is used to "make new seeds" and the sixth panel is revealed showing "pumpkin seeds"...and then there were none (please see the drawing below).

8. Shuffle, Bend, Slide, and Wave
By Sharon MacDonald

Shuffle to the left and shuffle to the right
And you snap, and snap, and snap, and snap.
A heel and a toe and turn yourself around
And a heel and a toe and, on you go!

Bend to the left and bend to the right
And you clap, and clap, and clap, and clap.
A heel and a toe and turn yourself around
And a heel and a toe and, on you go!

Slide to left and slide to the right
And you stomp and stomp and stomp and stomp.
A heel and a toe and turn yourself around
And a heel and a toe and, on you go.

Wave to the left and wave to the right
And you walk and walk and walk and walk.
A heel and a toe and turn yourself around
And a heel and a toe and sit back down.

Activities

1. As the children say the poem, do the movements. Model shuffling and sliding, if necessary, since a few of them may not know how to do them. When you say, "And a heel and a toe and on you go!" **you** do the heel and toe movement; then the children take about six forward steps and say, "and, on you go!"

2. If some of the children don't know left from right, tie a ribbon, a crepe paper streamer, or a piece of yarn around their left wrists. You can also make a left-handed Popsicle stick "hand" for each child to hold. Copy the picture below and glue it to a Popsicle stick, like the picture directions show below. Cut two horizontal slits about 2" long and ½" apart. Slip the Popsicle stick through the slits and glue it to the back of the hand sign.

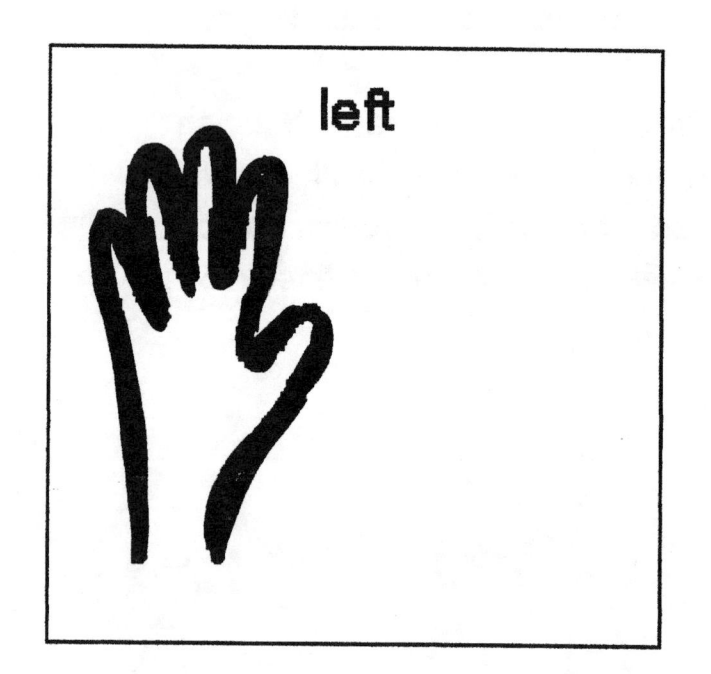

3. Make a poster of the poem. Put a piece of soft-side Velcro beside each verse. Copy, color, and cut out the pictures that show the movements in the poem. Back them with construction paper and laminate them. Put a small piece of hook-side Velcro on the back of each picture. The children match the pictures to the movements.

NOTE: if the poem is too long to write on a sheet of poster board, use an old window shade. That will give you much more room for writing the entire song.

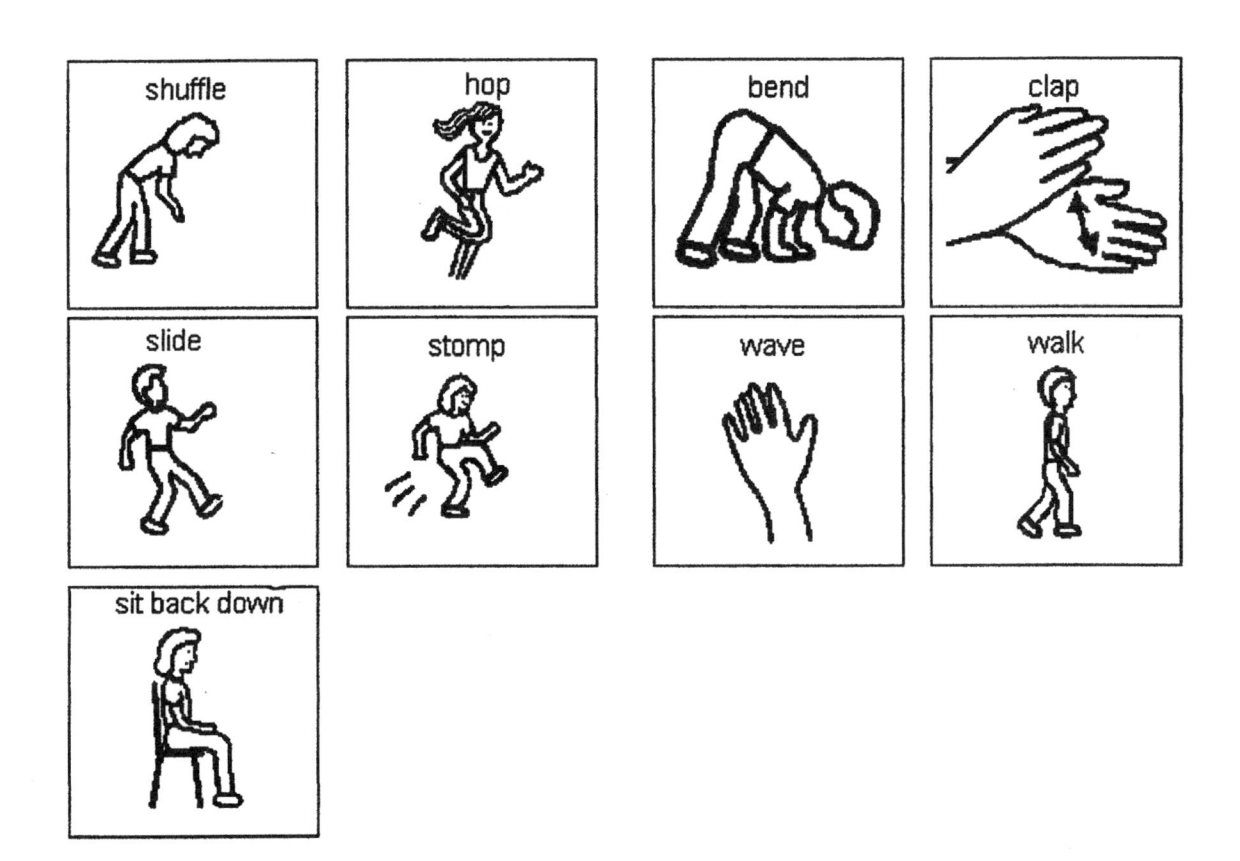

shuffle	hop	bend	clap
slide	stomp	wave	walk
sit back down			

5. Have the children think of other movements they could do instead of the ones in the poem. Maybe they could: "wiggle to the left and hop, and, hop, and hop, and hop"; or, they could "jump, or crawl, or point."

58

9. Little Tree House
By Sharon MacDonald

Please build for me
A house in a tree
Called the little tree house,
The little tree house.

I'd like to be
In a house in a tree
Called the little tree house,
The little tree house.

Simplest thing.
There isn't much to it.
You just climb a tree
And nail everything to it.

I'd like it so,
Wherever I'd go,
I'd sing of my
Little tree house.

Activities

1. Use the following movements with the poem.

Repeat the following movements throughout the poem as you say it:

> Tap your knees with your hands two times.
> Clap your hands two times.
> Right-hand snap; then, clap your hands; left-hand snap; then clap your hands;
> Touch your nose with your right hand; then, reach across your body to touch your left shoulder.
> With your left hand, touch your nose; then, reach across to touch your right shoulder.
> Touch your thumbs to your fingers three times

2. Make a poster of the poem. Using highlighter tape, cover the word "tree" each time you find it in the poem.

3. Put out a folder of drawing paper and a basket of markers, or crayons. Encourage the children to draw a tree house.

4. Make a paper-lunch-bag tree, follow the directions below. In the fall of the year, glue fall-colored leaves to the tree; in the winter, cover it with liquid glue and sprinkle plastic snow on the branches; in the spring, glue green leaves, or apple blossoms, on the branches. You can make a big tree with a large grocery bag. Attach alphabet letters to the bag similar to what they suggest you do in the book, Chica Chica Boom Boom, by Bill Martin Jr. and John Archambault.

Tree-making directions:

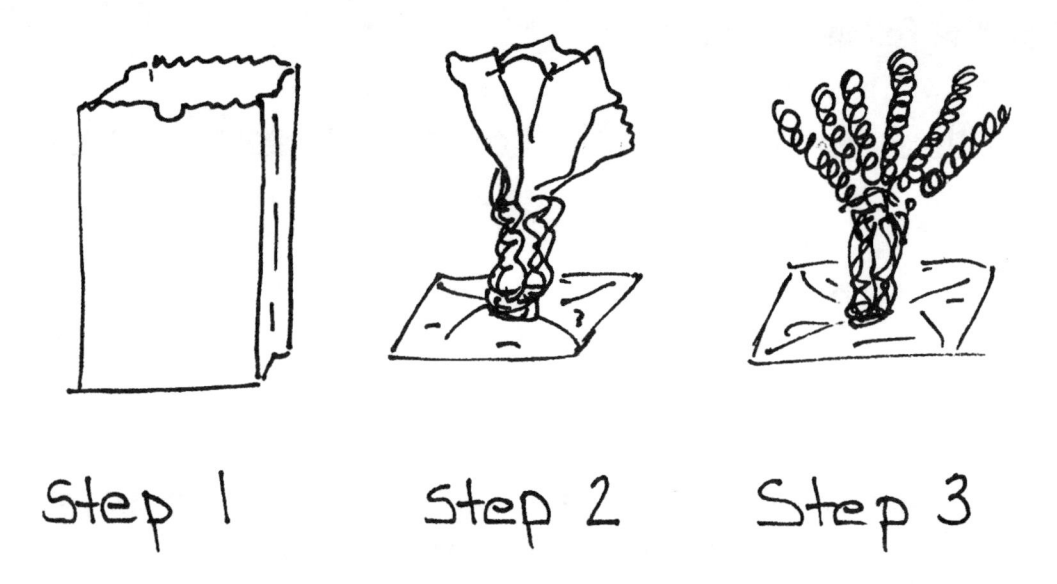

Step 1   Step 2   Step 3

Note: When I use trees in the block center, I put a tablespoon of sand in a snack-sized plastic baggie, zip and tape it closed. I put the baggie in the bottom of the paper tree to improve its stability.

I want to extend a special note of thanks to Dr. Jean Feldman for this activity.

5. Problem-solving can be taught by using the paper lunch-bag tree making activity. How? By challenging the children to build a tree house, that will sit in their paper tree, using these materials: jumbo craft sticks, bottle caps, twigs, fabric, left-over laminating film, aluminum foil, paper clips, wax paper, brown grocery-bag paper, construction paper, and other paper products you have on hand.

6. Have a fruit-tasting party, using fruits and nuts that grow on trees.

    Collect: Fruits and nuts
           large serving tray
           small plate
           nut cracker
           knives.

Have each of the children bring to school something edible that grows on a tree. Be sure to have enough for each child to have a taste. Ask the children to prepare for their party by cutting the fruit into small pieces and cracking the nuts with a nutcracker (**supervise these activities closely**). Place the fruits and nuts on trays. Ask each child to count the pieces to make sure they have enough for everyone to have a taste. The children fill their plates with samples of the fruits and nuts and they taste them. Ask each child to guess on which tree the tree fruit grows.

7. Take the children outside do a bark rubbing of the trees near the school. The children place the paper on the bark and, using the side of the crayon, rub back and forth over the paper on the bark. Collect many rubbings from different trees. When you return to the classroom, compare the different rubbings.

8. Collect and compare seeds from seed-producing trees around your neighborhood or school. You will need seeds from trees that produce them, a lunch bag for each child, and 5-6 shoeboxes.

Give each child a lunch bag and take the children on a tree-seed collecting walk around the school. What you collect will depend on what trees are around. The best time of the year to collect is in autumn when the seeds typically fall to the ground. When you return to the classroom, place the shoeboxes on the floor. Have the children put the seeds in the shoeboxes (let them decide how best to group them). As a suggestion to help with the sorting and comparing, if you collect five types of seeds, limit the number of shoeboxes to three. The children will then have to select criteria by which to group the seeds. Talk about how the seeds are alike. Some examples of seed categories are nuts, bean-like seeds, sticky seeds, and seeds with "wings" that fly when they fall.

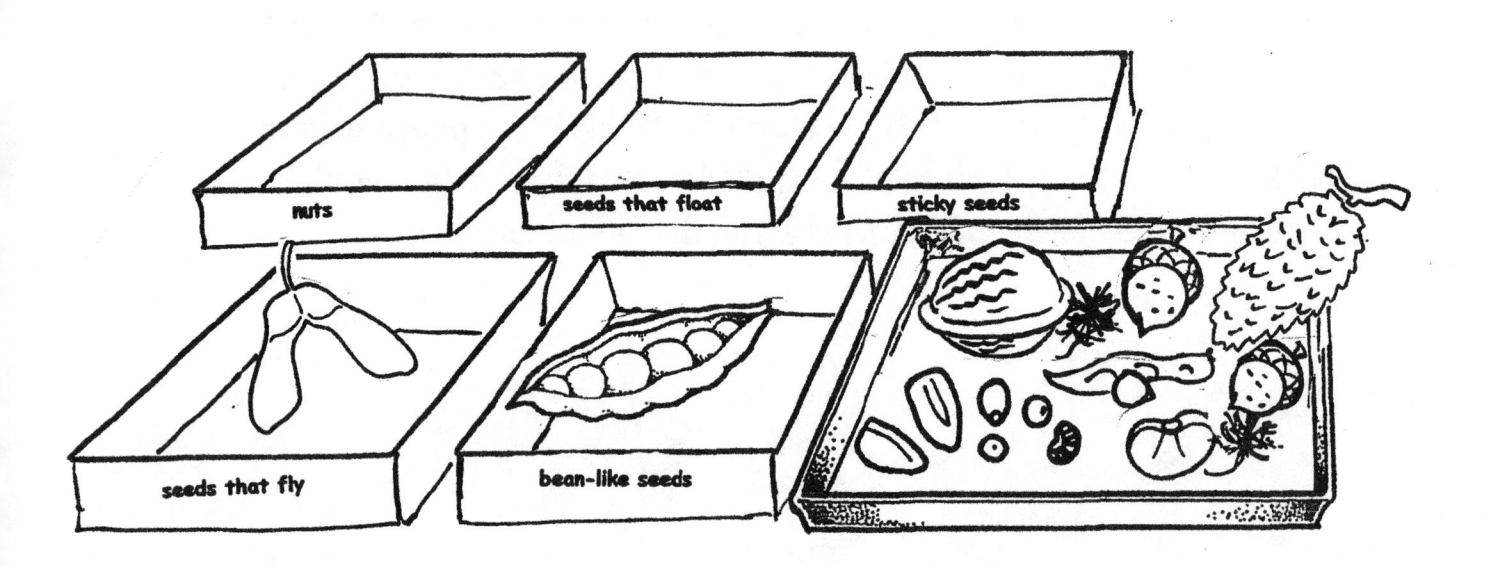

10. I Can't Spell Ohio!
By Sharon MacDonald

I can spell *cat*, "c" "a" "t."
I can spell *bat*, "b" "a" "t."
I can spell *hat*, "h" "a" "t."
But I can't spell *Ohio*.

"O" is on the front side
And "O" is at the end.
I don't know what in the middle
I guess I'll ask my friend.

I can spell *dog*, "d" "o" "g."
I can spell *hog*, "h" "o" "g."
I can spell *log*, "l" "o" "g."
But I can't spell *Ohio*.

"O" is on the front side
And "O" is at the end.
I don't know what in the middle
I guess I'll ask my friend.

I can spell *fig*, "f" "i" "g."
I can spell *pig*, "p" "i" "g."
I can spell *wig*, "w" "i" "g."
But I can't spell *Ohio*.

"O" is on the front side
And "O" is at the end.
And "HI" is in the middle,
It's how I greet my friend.

I can spell *cat*, "c" "a" "t."
I can spell *bat*, "b" "a" "t."
I can spell *hat*, "h" "a" "t."
And I can spell *Ohio*.
Yes, I can spell Ohio..."O," "H," "I," "O."

Activities

1. Make a poster of the poem with plastic pockets over the all the words that make up the three word families (e.g., "cat," "bat," "hat"). To make the pockets, cut strips of leftover laminating film slightly longer the word and apply clear-plastic tape to attach the film over the word. Put the tape along the bottom and each side of the laminating film (please see the directions below).

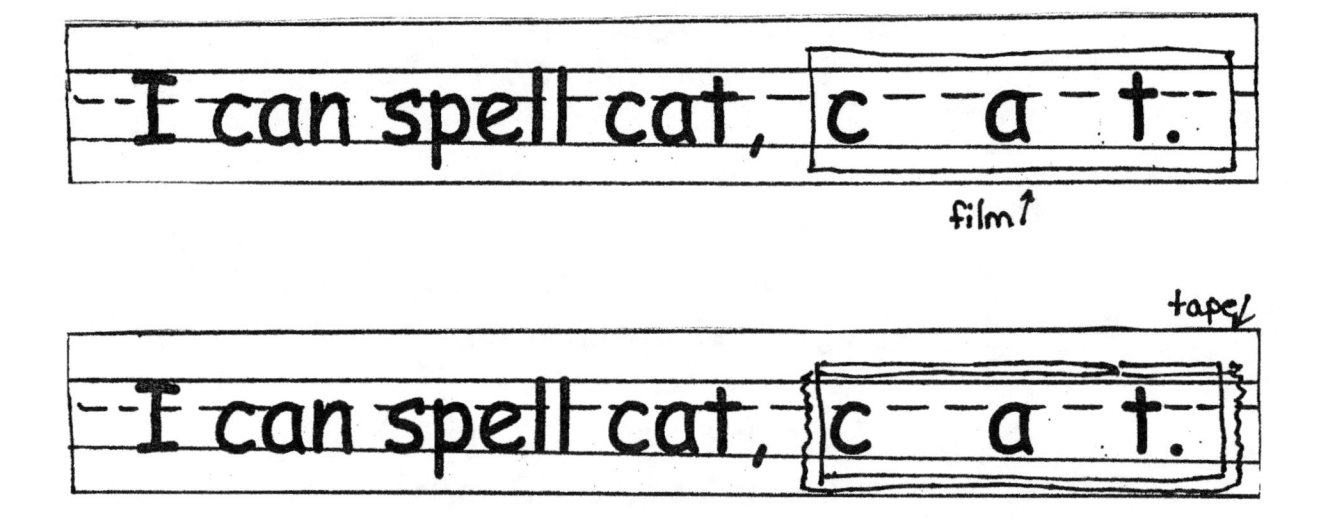

I can spell cat, c a t.
film ↑

I can spell cat, c a t.
tape ↙

Copy, color, and cut out the pictures on page 66. Make them stiffer by backing them with tag board; laminate them. The children will match the picture to the words they spelled by slipping the picture into the laminating-film pocket over the word.

cat	bat	hat
dog	pig	log
wig	hog	fig

2. To make this a matching activity, put each letter (e.g., "c," "a," "t") of each word on a short sentence strip. Put these in a basket for the children to match to the words they are learning to spell in the poem.

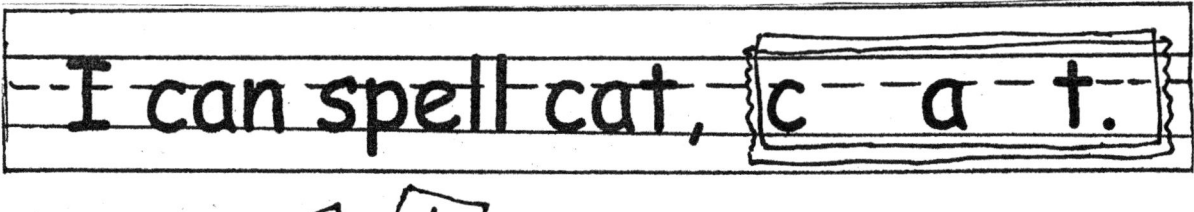

I can spell cat, c a t.

3. Make his activity more challenging by making the poem poster differently. In the place where the spelled words go, leave blanks. Attach laminating film pockets over the blank spaces. The children find the letters you made in Activity 2, spell the word, and then put the letters in the laminating-film pockets (please see below).

4. Make a word tray like the one below. Use the die cut to make the letters in the word "Ohio." Put all the letters in a small basket beside the word tray. The children put the word "Ohio" together. You can also do it with the word families in the poem.

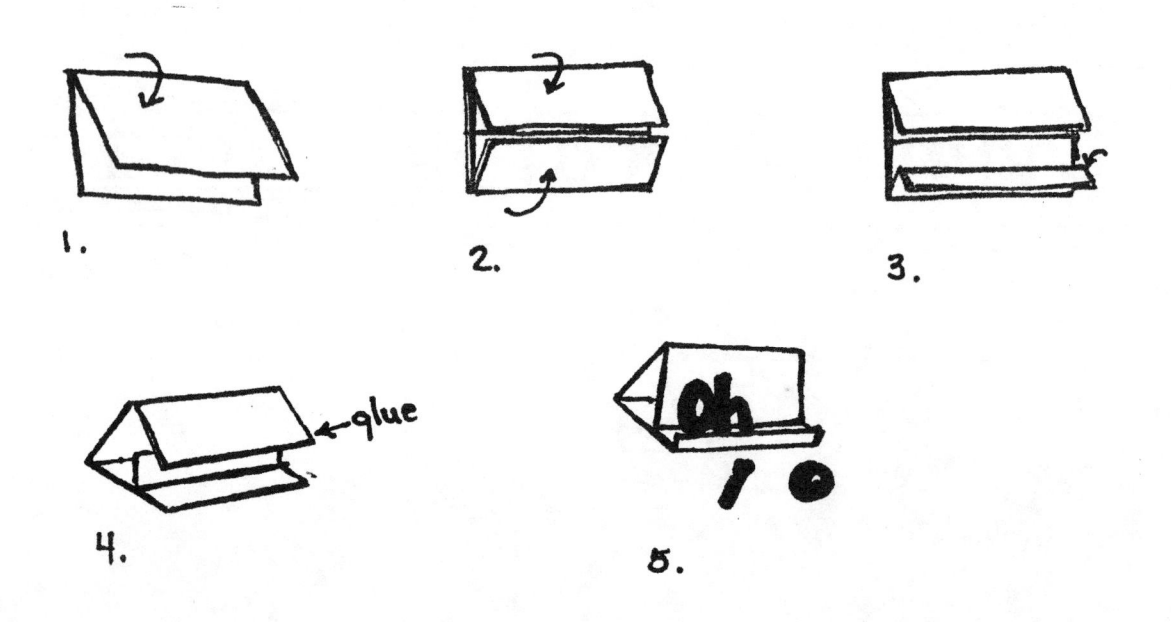

1.

2.

3.

4. ←glue

5.

5. Divide the class into three groups. Group 1 will be the "at" family, Group 2 will be the "og" family, Group 3 will be the "ig" family. When you say the word, the children from that word family group spell the word. For example, when you say, "cat", the children from Group 1 say, "c," "a," "t."

6. Make eight-panel flipbooks with your children. You begin the task by writing the three words in the word family on the first three panels of the flipbook, for example, the "at" family (please see the picture directions below). Then, draw the picture for each of the words on the concealed panels underneath the each of the words you wrote. Show the children the words and have them guess what it is. Then lift the panel to see the picture and check if they are correct. On the fourth panel the child writes a word that rhymes with the first three words, then draws the picture of the word on the concealed panel beneath the word.

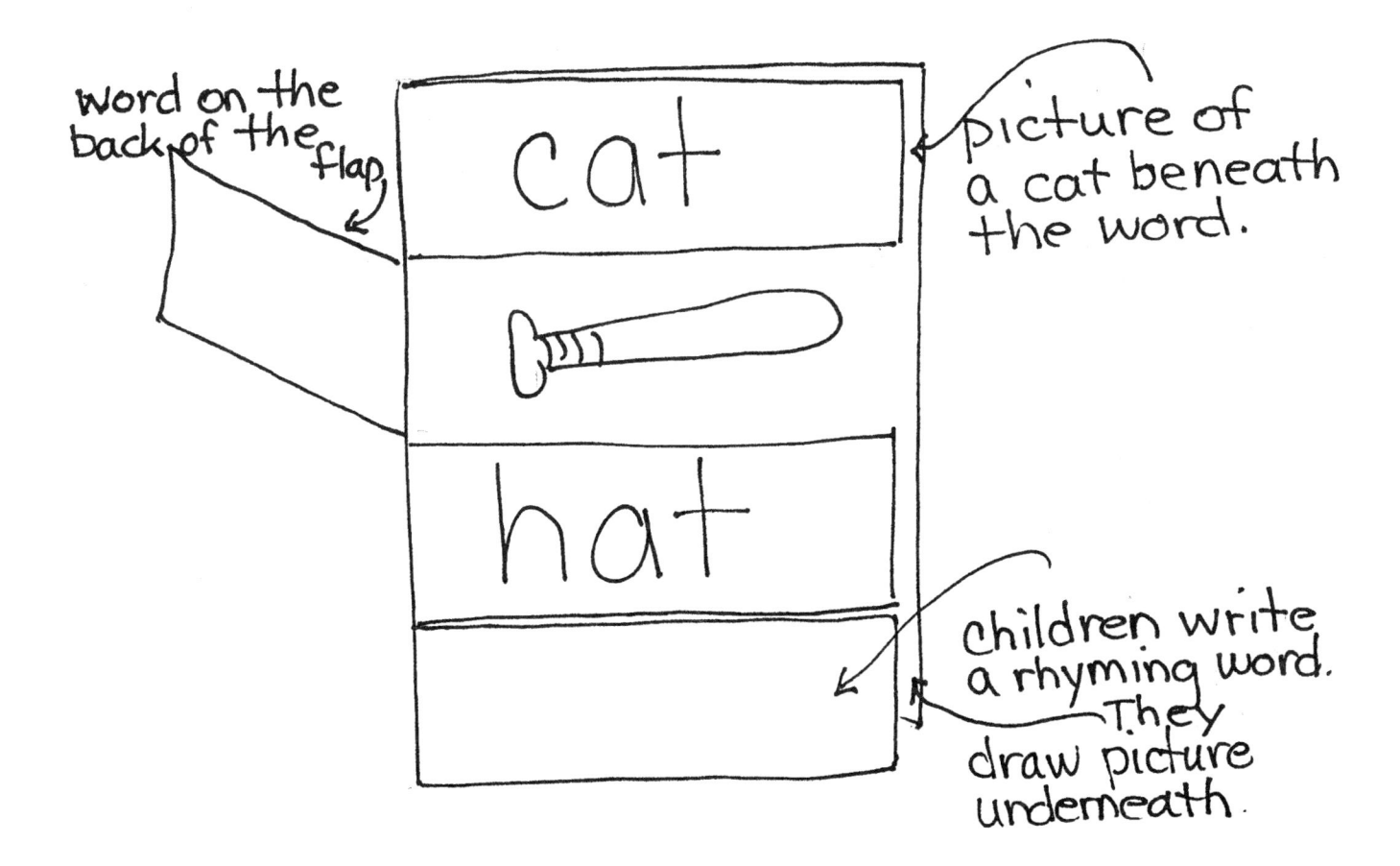

word on the back of the flap

cat

picture of a cat beneath the word.

hat

children write a rhyming word. They draw picture underneath.

7. After the children have worked with the poem and understand the three-word families, make "word-family" cans. Use three clean orange juice cans, and nine jumbo craft sticks. Cover the cans with paper and write: "at" family on one can, "og" family on another can, and "ig" family on the last can. Write the words from the poem on the craft sticks; as the children read the words from the word families, they place the sticks in the correct word-family can.

8. Make a paper bag, word-family book. Use nine small, brown lunch bags, glue, a black marker, three large notebook rings, and the pictures from Activity 1 above. On the front of the first three bags write a word from one of the word families. On the first bag, "cat," on the second, "bat," and on the third, "hat." Glue the picture of the word under each of the bag-flaps. If the child doing the activity cannot read the word, he lifts the flap to see the picture of the word. Place a small plastic cat, bat, or hat inside the bag to help the child further in learning to read the word. Use the notebook ring to put the three paper bags together. Do this all the word families in the poem. See the directions on page 70.

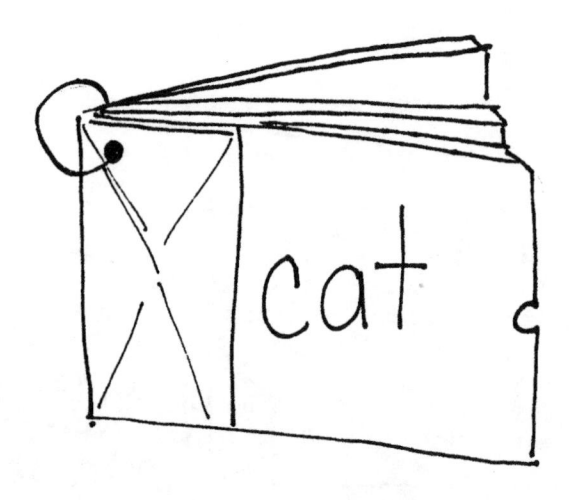

Lunch Bag Books:

1. Use three lunch bags, a plastic representation of the word on the bag, a picture of the word on the bag, a hole punch, glue, and a notebook ring.

2. Write the word (e.g., cat) on the lunch bag.

3. Glue the picture of the word beneath the flap.

4. Place the plastic representation of the word inside the lunch bag.

5. Hold the bag closed, put hook-side *Velcro* on one side of the open bag, soft-side *Velcro* on the other. The children can open and close the bag without the objects inside falling out.

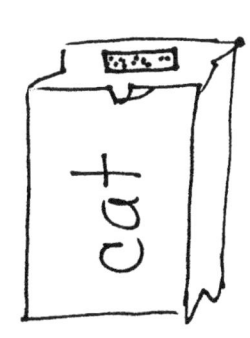

6. Make a hole in the upper left-hand corner of the bag using the hole punch.

7. Slide the ring into each hole.

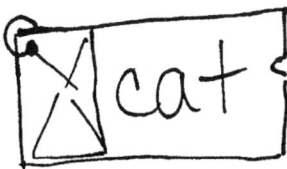

11. Triangles, Bells, Sticks, and Maracas
By Sharon MacDonald

When we play our instruments softly
We make a musical sound.
Triangles, triangles,
Make a beautiful sound.

When we play our instruments softly
We make a musical sound.
Bells, bells,
Make a beautiful sound.

When we play our instruments softly
We make a musical sound.
Sticks, sticks
Make a beautiful sound.

When we play our instruments softly
We make a musical sound.
Maracas, maracas,
Make a beautiful sound.

When we play them all together
We make a musical sound.
Triangles, bells, sticks, maracas,
Make a big band sound.

Activities

1. Make a poster of the poem. With a hole-punch, make holes along the edge of the poster next to each verse. Push brads through the holes with the legs extending through the back of the poster. Let the

brad heads stand off from the poster-face so objects can be hung from the heads, then open the legs of the brad, in rear of the poster, and tape them in place.

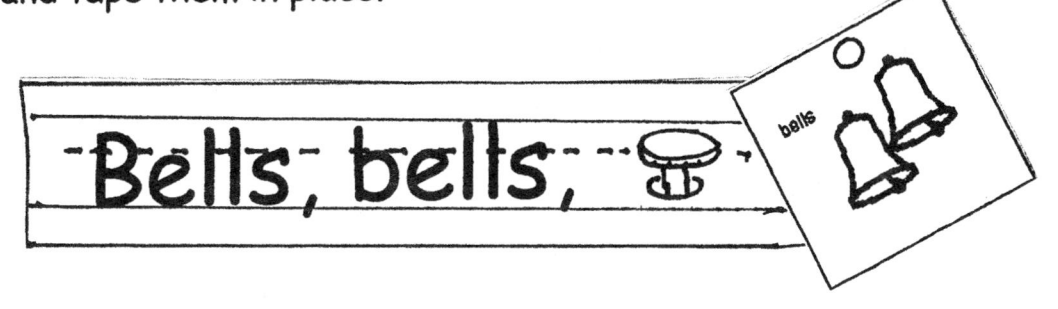

Bells, bells,

Copy, color, and cut out the pictures below. Back them with construction paper and laminate them. Punch holes at the top of the pictures. The children match the pictures to the verses by placing the picture over the heads of the brads.

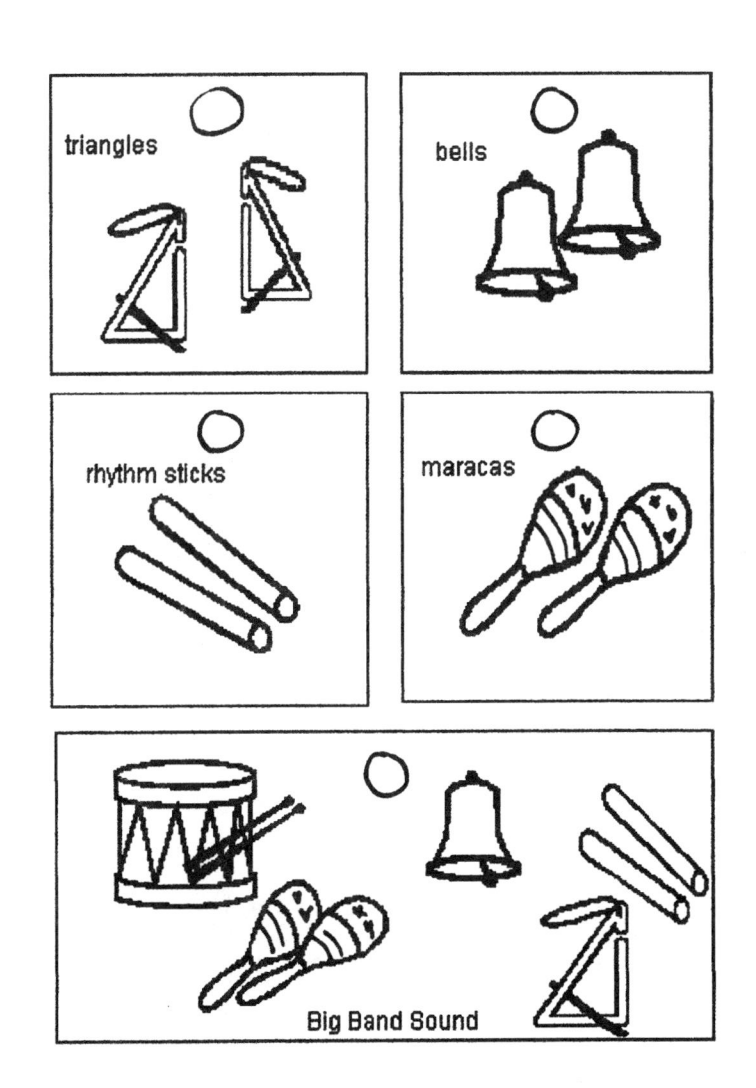

triangles

bells

rhythm sticks

maracas

Big Band Sound

72

Make this activity more challenging for older children by writing the names of the instruments on short sentence strips. Punch holes in the top of the strips. The children match the sentence strips to the names of the instruments in the poem.

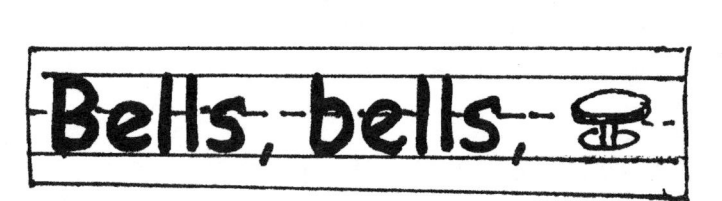

2. As you say the poem, use the instruments. See the instructions below to make each instrument.

Triangles: Use horseshoes and the longest nails you can find. File the sharp ends off the nails. Use the nails as strikers.

Bells: Collect different size bells. Tie ribbon to the ends of each bell.

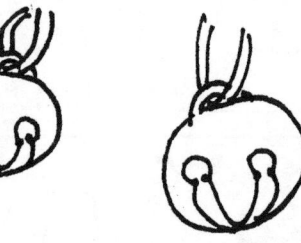

Sticks: Cut an old broom handle into several 9"-12" lengths. Sand the ends smooth to remove the splinters.

Maracas: Use several small plastic jars with lids. Put a few coins in one, pebbles in another, and buttons in the last one. Put on the lids with *Super Glue*. Decorate the jar.

3. If you do not want to make instruments, use the ones you have on hand. Substitute the instrument names in the poem with the ones you have and let the children play.

4. Copy, color, and cut out the pictures below. Back them with construction paper and laminate them. Have the children sort them by the categories of instruments that: are blown, struck, and strummed with the fingers.

guitar	harmonica	horn
piano	rhythm sticks	cymbals
drum	cello	triangle

12. Fruit Salad
By Sharon MacDonald

Bananas, pears and strawberries, too.
Pineapples, peaches, and kiwis for you.
Cantaloupes, apples, and mangos will do
Let's make a fruit salad for you, and you.
Honeydews, grapes, and blackberries, too.
Raspberries, raisins, and figs for you.
Plums, and prunes, and cherries will do
Let's make a fruit salad for you and you.

Activities

1. Write each line of the poem on a sentence strip. Copy, color, cut out, back with construction paper, and laminate the pictures below. The children put the sentence strips in a pocket chart in the order that they occur in the poem. They match the picture to the name of the fruit.

apples   peaches   raisins

cherries   pineapples   plums

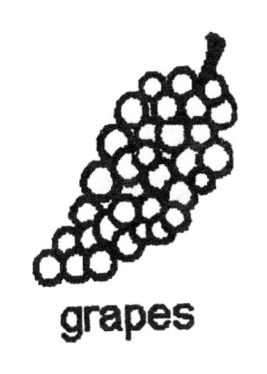

grapes	pears	cantaloupes
strawberries	honeydews	kiwis
figs	blackberries	raspberries
bananas	mangos	prunes

After the children have mastered putting the poem together, encourage them to put it together in a different order and read it; or challenge a friend to read it.

2. Put drawing paper, crayons, and markers in a basket under the poem poster. Have the children draw other fruits that could go in a fruit salad. Use the fruits they draw to make a new verse to the poem.

3. Use the pictures above to graph the fruits by size, color, how they grow (for example: a vine, a tree, a bush), or what their seeds look like.

4. Make a fruit salad.

5. Alphabetize the fruits in the poem. Put a chart on the wall with the letters A through Z listed as shown below. Have the children find all the "A" fruits in the poem, then the "B" fruits, and so on. Write their dictation on the chart as shown. Do all of the fruits in the poem. (Have the children try to find fruits that start with other letters of the alphabet.)

A: Apple	O:
B: Bananas, blackberries	P: Peaches, pears, pineapple, plums, prunes
C: Cantaloupe, cherries	
D:	Q:
E:	R: Raisins, raspberries
F: Figs	S: Strawberries
G: Grapes	T:
H: Honeydews	U:
I:	V:
J:	W:
K: Kiwi	X:
L:	Y:
M: Mangos	Z:
N:	

77

6. Make a fruit wheel. Include all of the fruits in the poem. The children will turn the wheel as they say the poem.

Here's how to make the fruit wheel. Use two pizza circles. On one of the circles glue the pictures of the fruits in the order that they occur in the poem. Space them evenly apart around the edge of the wheel. On the second pizza circle, cut out a square opening that would allow one picture of a fruit at a time to show from the bottom circle as the top pizza circle turns over the top of it. Make a hole in the center of the two circles; insert a brad, fold down the legs to hold the circles together. As the children say the fruit, they turn the wheel to show the picture of the fruit.

Fruit Salad Wheel

Fruit Salad Wheel

79

7. **Make a three-cube spelling game.** Make three copies on card stock of the cube found on page 81. Use the 18 pictures of the fruits in the poem from Activity 1; glue each picture to the six sides of the three cubes. The children roll their cube until it stops. They spell the fruit picture showing on the top of the cube. The children use die-cut or magnet letters to spell the words.

Note: I usually stuff tissue paper in each cube. It makes it less likely that the cubes will get crushed.

80

glue glue

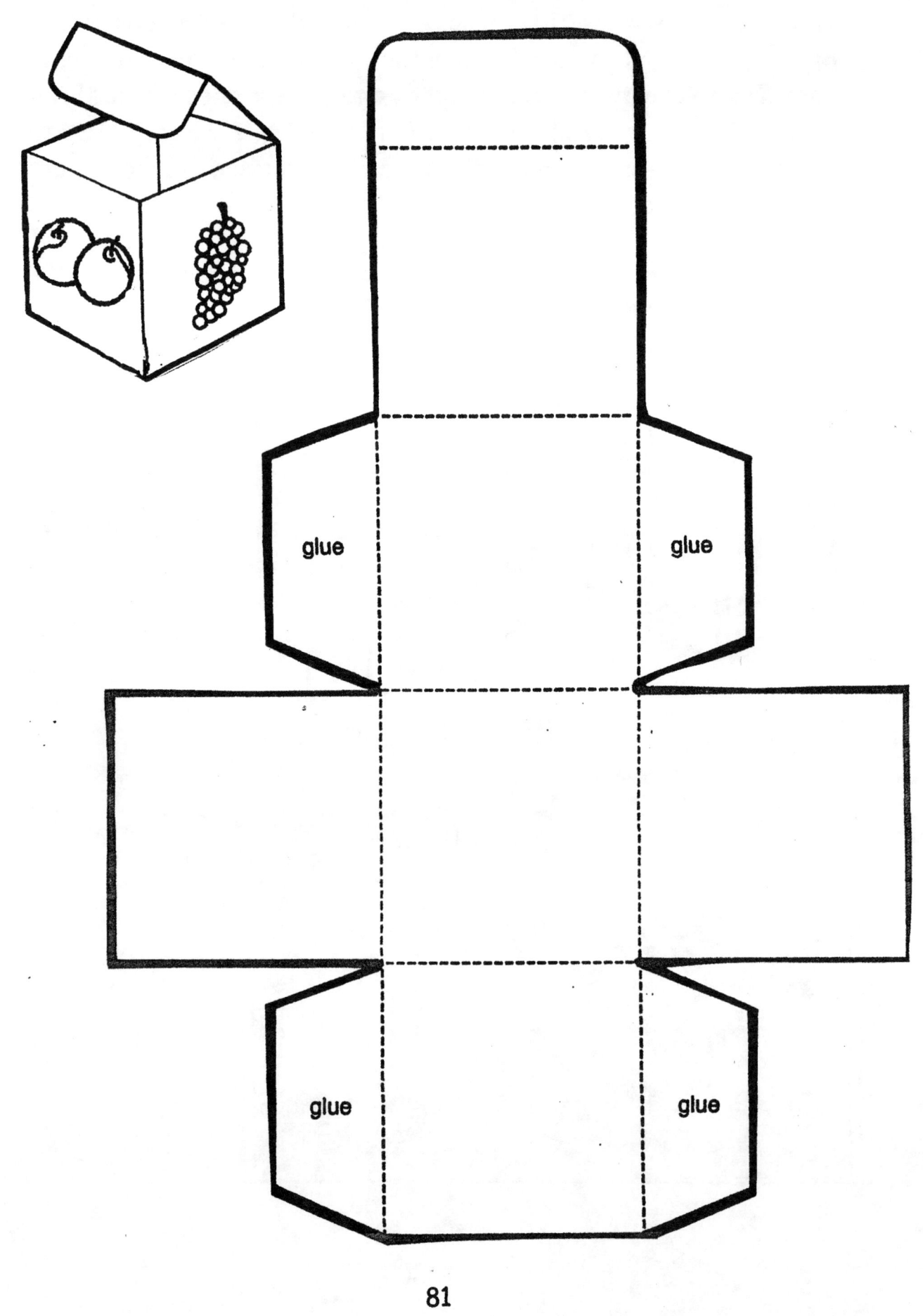

glue glue

13. The Scissors' Song
By Sharon MacDonald

I have a pair of scissor
I'd like to learn to use.
They have two holes for fingers.
Which ones? I'll have to choose.
I open and I close 'em
To make the scissors go.
But just to cut the paper
I've got to hold just soooooooo.

Snip, snip, is the clip I'd like to learn.
Snip, snip is the clip when I have my turn.
Snip, snip is sound when the scissors cut.
Snip, snip is the scissors' song.

The blades do all the cutting.
That's how I must begin.
But someone else must show me
How to keep the paper in.
The blades go up and down,
As I try to cut a line
I keep my fingers in the holes
"Thumbs Up" I say each time.

Snip, snip is the clip I'd like to learn.
Snip, Snip is the clip when I have my turn.
Snip, snip is sound when the scissors cut.
Snip, snip is the scissors' song.

Activities

1. Make a poster of the poem. Use highlighter tape; the children highlight all the words that say, "snip."

2. Print each line of the chorus on a separate sentence strip. Have the children put the lines in a pocket chart in the order that they occur in the poem.

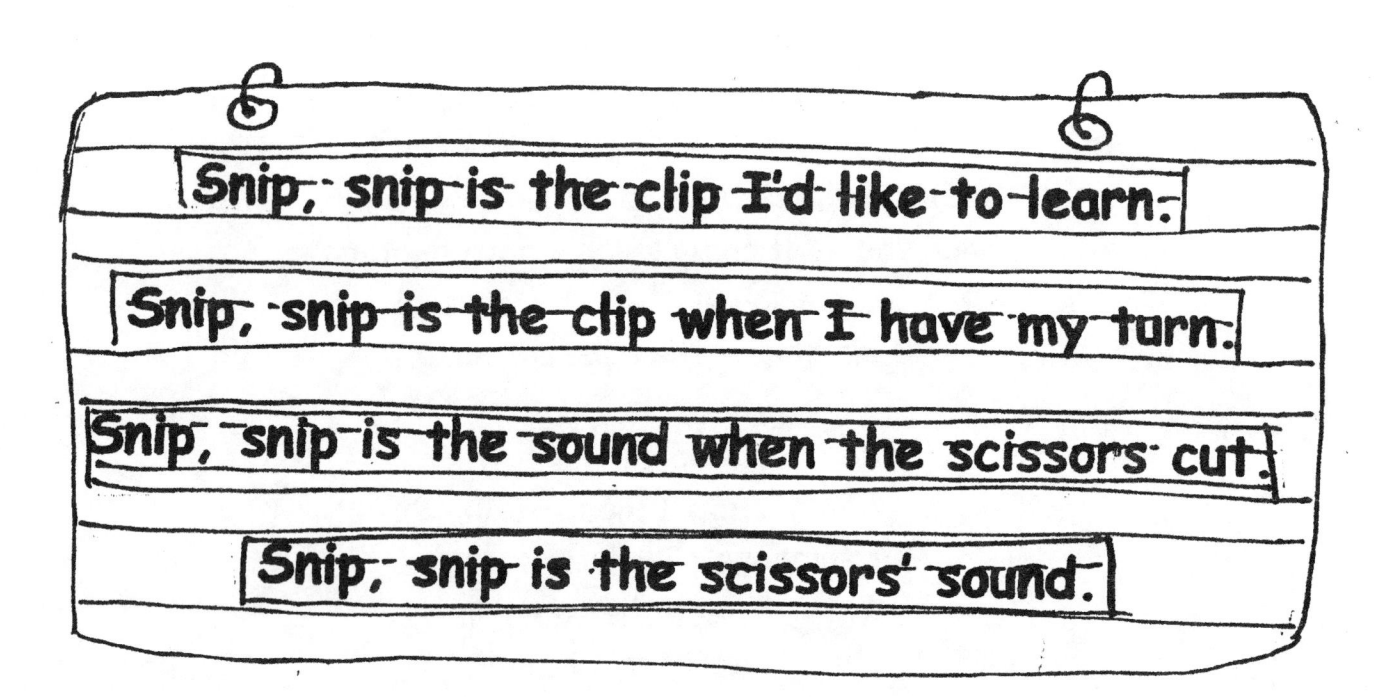

> Snip, snip is the clip I'd like to learn.
>
> Snip, snip is the clip when I have my turn.
>
> Snip, snip is the sound when the scissors cut.
>
> Snip, snip is the scissors' sound.

After the children have mastered putting the lines of the poem in proper order, have them put the lines in a different order and read the poem that way.

3. Use *Wikki Stiks* to outline the initial consonant *blends* like: "sn," "cl," "sc," "bl," and the initial consonant *digraphs* like: "sh," "ch," and "th."

4. Place a folder of white copier paper and scissors in a basket in an Art area. Have the children use one sheet of paper to cut stair steps from the paper. Ask them to count their snips. Have them use four snips to cut a stop sign. See if they can cut a house using two snips and with four snips, cut a butterfly. For younger children, see if they can cut a triangle, a square, and a rectangle. As they cut, have them count their snips.

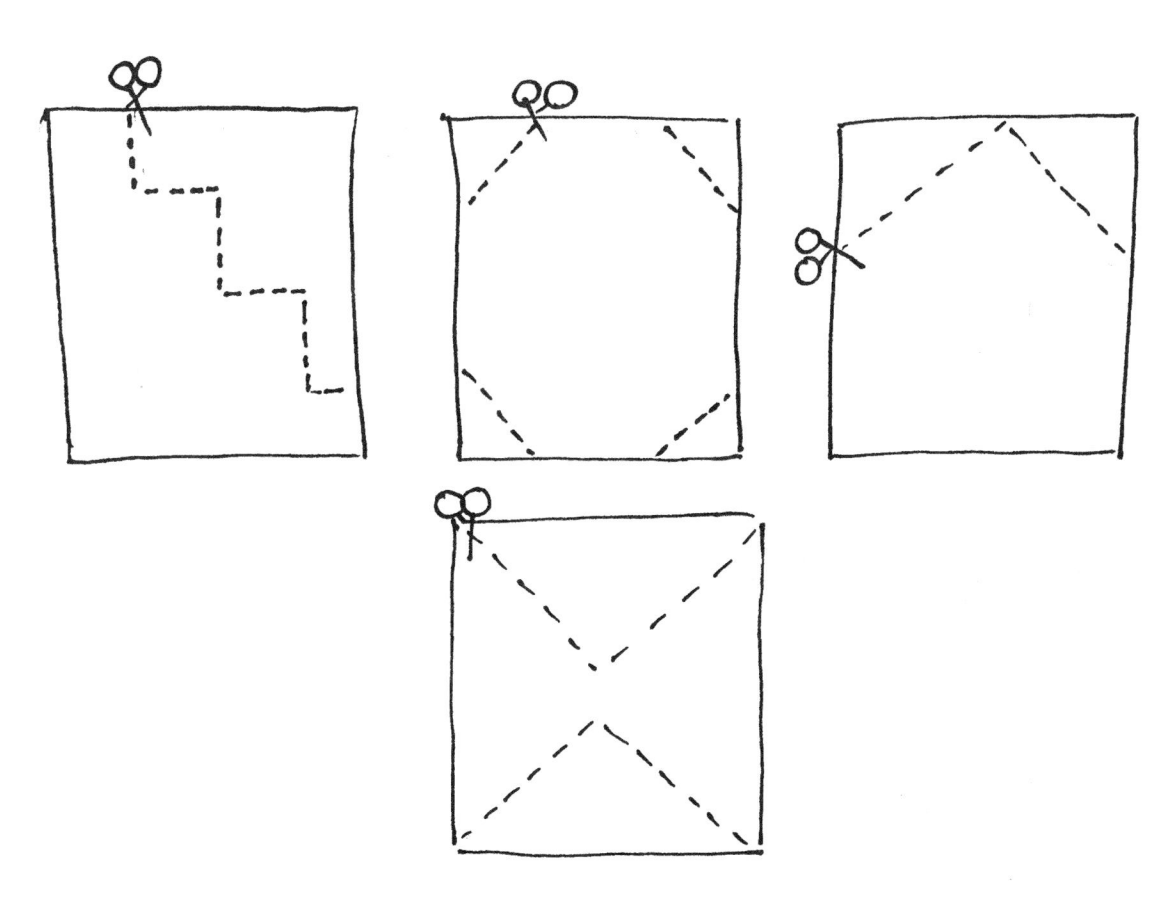

5. Have the children make a list of shapes they could cut with the scissors. Post the list on the wall. Leave space for them to add to the list when they think of another shape.

6. Have the children do "strip-snipping" as they say the poem. Place pre-cut 2" x 8" strips of construction paper in a basket on the art table. Give the children scissors, a few strips, and small brown lunch bags to put their strips in. As they say the poem, have them cut the strips into smaller pieces. When they have finished, have them use the snips to make a collage.

Strip Snipping

1. Put the paper in the scissors.

2. Close the scissors.

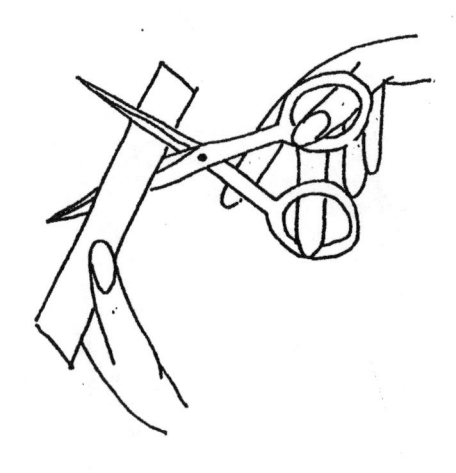

3. Cut the paper apart.

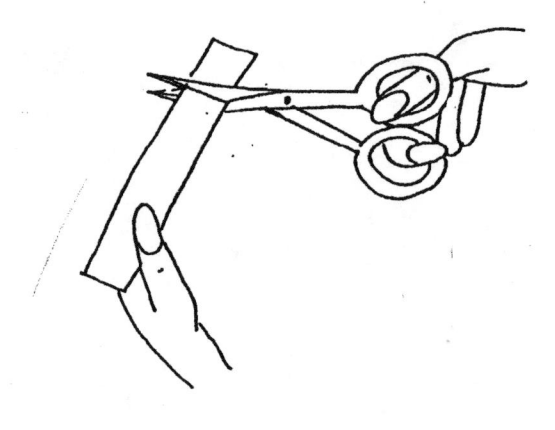

4. Put the pieces in the bag.

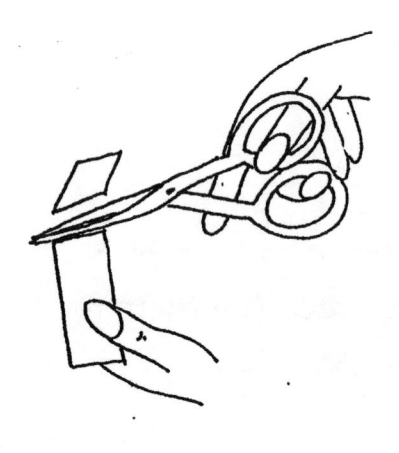

7. Make a Scissor Book for each child (or have them make their own) using a layered book (like the one below). Write a line of the chorus on each of the four tabs. The children use their scissor work to decorate each line of the poem. Have the children use the strips they cut in Activity 6 above, or use the shapes they cut in Activity 4, to illustrate each page of the book.

Layered Book:

1. Stack two sheets of copier paper, with the back sheet 1" higher than the one on the top.

2. Fold the bottom of both pages upward and place the edges so that all the layers are the same distance apart.

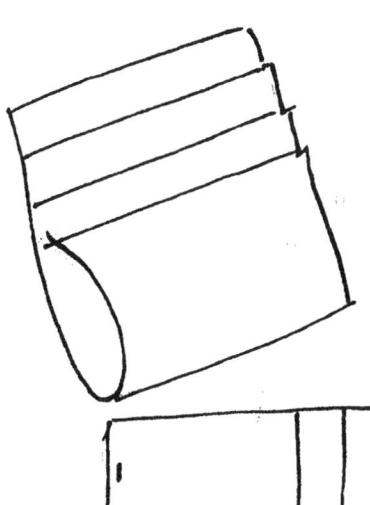

3. Staple them together at the top.

4. Write each line of the chorus on each page at the bottom.

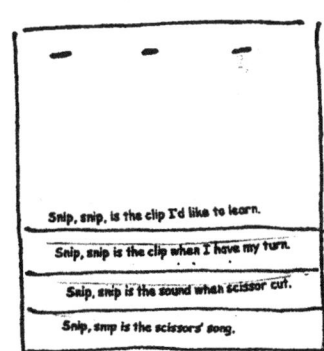

14. What's On A Face?
By Sharon MacDonald

What's on a face, what do you see there?
Two ears that hear, and a head with some hair,
Two eyes with lashes that see and blink,
And two furry eyebrows that wiggle, I think.

There's only one nose pushed outward to smell.
It does sneezes, which it does quite well.
There are two lips that nibble around.
Lips up say, "Smile." Lips down, say, "Frown."

Some faces are round while others are square.
Most faces say what our feelings put there.
Smiles, and grins, frowns and droopy chins.
Feelings...are what our faces wear.

There are two cheeks at each end of a grin.
And the face stops at a point called the chin.
Two puffy cheeks at the end of a smile,
Then, the face stops; it's the face of a child.

Activities

1. Make a picture-word puzzle-match. Use the pictures and the names of the parts of the face shown below. The children match the words to the picture parts of the face.

smile or grin   cheek   chin   lips

nose   eyebrow   eyes   ears   hair

2. Take a photograph of each of your children's faces. Duplicate and laminate them and, if possible, enlarge them. Use one of the photographs for a puzzle base; let the children cut the second photograph into puzzle pieces. The children work the puzzle on the base that is their face. Store the base and puzzle pieces in an envelope or in a plastic baggie.

3. Collect a baby picture of each of the children in your class. Put in a basket the baby faces and the current photographs of faces (from Activity #2 above). The children match the photographs.

4. Make a poster of the poem. Have the children use highlighter tape to find the different facial expressions and the movements of various parts of the face.

5. Make a feeling chart with the pictures below.

happy	afraid	bored	disappointed
embarrassed	excited	frustrated	mad
proud	sad	surprised	tired
worried	shocked		

6. Bring a hand-mirror to school. One at a time, have the children look in the mirror and draw their face with permanent markers. Have them draw right on the mirror. Make the mirror ready for the next child by cleaning it with liquid window-cleaner.

7. A delightful book titled Make a Face, written by Henry and Amy Schwartz and published by Scholastic, has a Mylar mirror in the back of the book. It has the best facial expressions! Have your children try to make faces like the ones in the book.

8. Make a face puzzle using jumbo craft sticks. Give each child six sticks. You'll also need masking tape and colored markers. Tape the six sticks together side-by-side. Put strips of tape across the top and bottom of the sticks. Turn over the sticks so the tape is underneath. Make one set for each child. The children draw their faces with the markers on the set of taped sticks. When they have finished their faces, turn the taped sticks over and have the children number their sticks "1" to "6." Remove the tape. The children now have a stick puzzle they can put together and take apart. If they are having trouble reassembling their sticks, ask them to check the numbers on the back. All they need to do is put them together in number order, but maybe that is not as much fun!

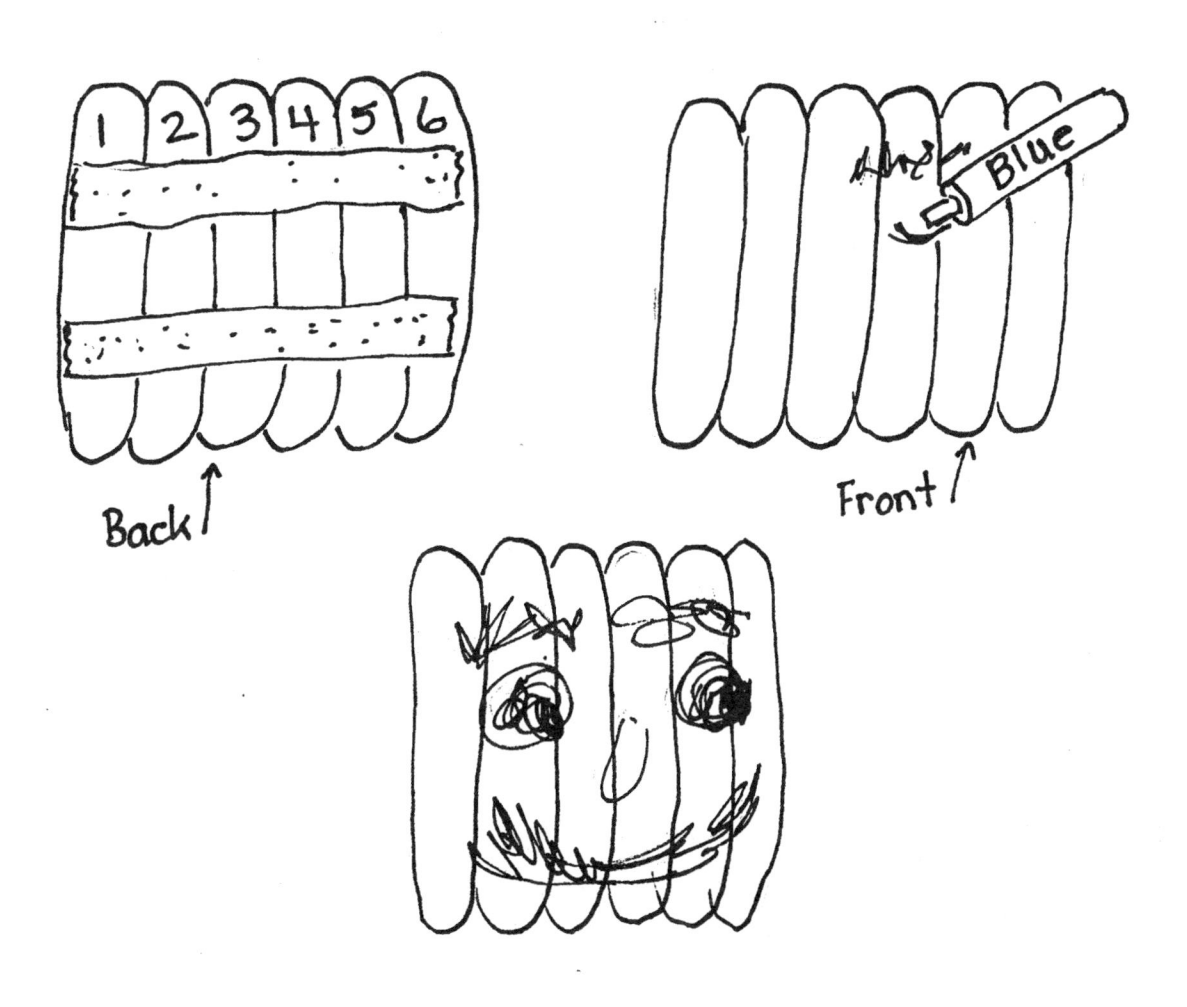

15. A Bare Foot Walker's Shoes
By Sharon MacDonald

I have shoes I use for hiking,
Flippers I wear to swim.
And tennies that grip me tightly
So I can climb the jungle gym.

I have ballet-dancing shoes,
Boots I wear to ride.
And shoes I use for skating
So I can roll and slide.

I have plastic boots for snow,
Floppy rubber ones for rain.
And sandals just for skipping
With my friends who skip the same!

Beneath my bed are flippers,
Slippers, boots, and shoes.
"What do I like to wear?"
"Barefoot is what I choose!"

Activities

1. Write the poem on sentence strips. Put the first two verses in a pocket chart. Copy, color, back with construction paper, cut out, and laminate the pictures on page 92. The children match the words in the poem to the shoe pictures. After the children have worked with the first two verses, put the last two verses in

the pocket chart and have them match the words and pictures again.

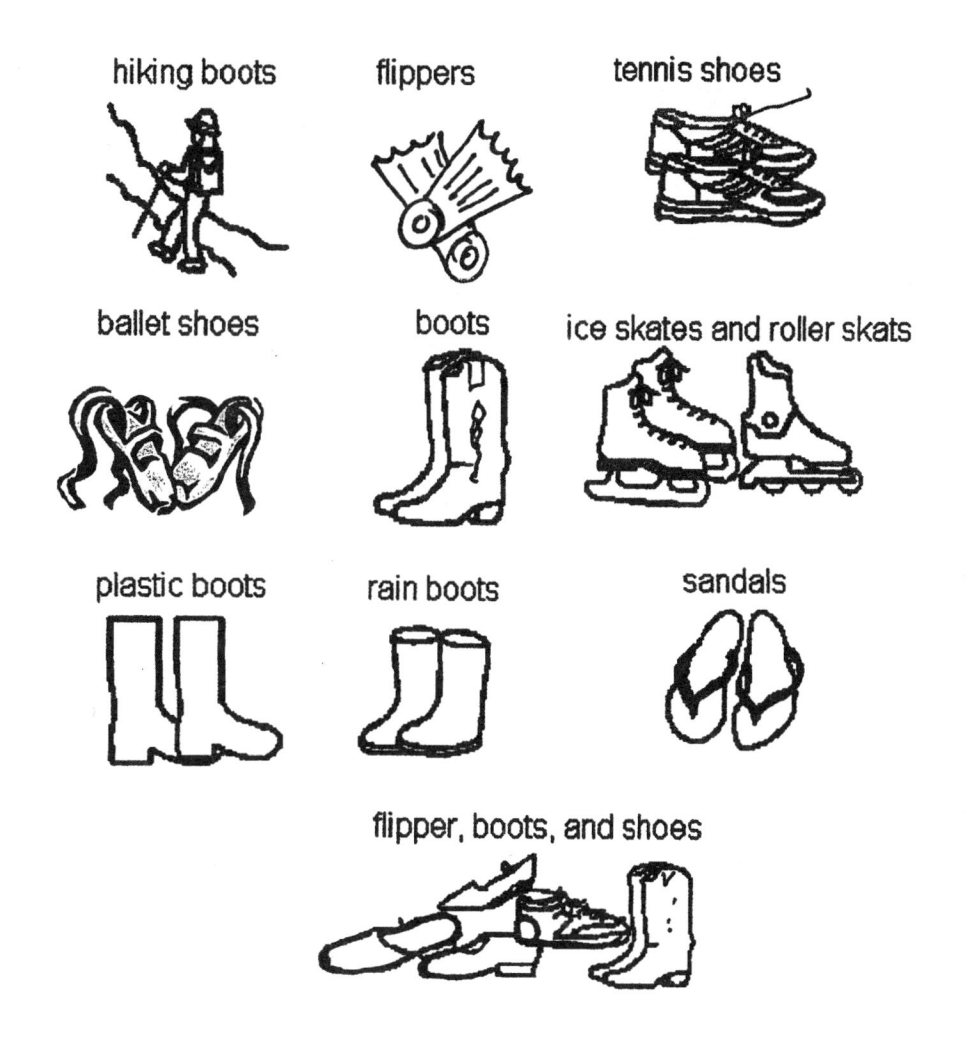

hiking boots   flippers   tennis shoes

ballet shoes   boots   ice skates and roller skats

plastic boots   rain boots   sandals

flipper, boots, and shoes

2. This is an excellent poem to work on punctuation with the children. It is helpful to attach movement to punctuation marks to improve their learning on page 93. Introduce the movements one at a time. When the children understand and use one movement, move on to the next.

Punctuation Made Memorable Through Movement

Question mark ("?")=Shrugs.
Comma (",")=Pause
Exclamation mark ("!")=One hand over the head
Capital letters ("CAPS")=Jump
Quotation marks ("")=Hold up and wiggle two fingers on each hand
Apostrophe (" ' ")=Hold up and wiggle the index finger
Period (".")=Stop

3. Provide the children with magazines that advertise shoes. Have them cut out all the shoe photographs and drawings that are mentioned in the poem. Make a shoe-word chart by cutting out a large shoe shape from brown butcher paper. Have the children glue to the brown butcher paper the shoe photographs and drawings they have found in magazines. If they can write, ask them to write the type of shoe under each photograph. If not, take their dictation about each shoe they found.

4. Use highlighter tape to underline the initial consonant blends: "cl," "pl," "sl," "fl," and "sk" and the initial consonant digraphs: "sh" and "ch."

5. Have the children dramatize the movements of the shoes as they do the different activities and tasks in the poem.

6. Collect an assortment of shoes from the children. Have the children sort them by work, play, and work-and-play. To do it, draw a Venn diagram on a large sheet of paper; tape the paper to the floor. In the left-hand side of the diagram write "WORK"; in the center write "WORK AND PLAY"; on the right-hand side

write "PLAY" (please see below). The children place the shoes in the part of the Venn diagram they think is appropriate.

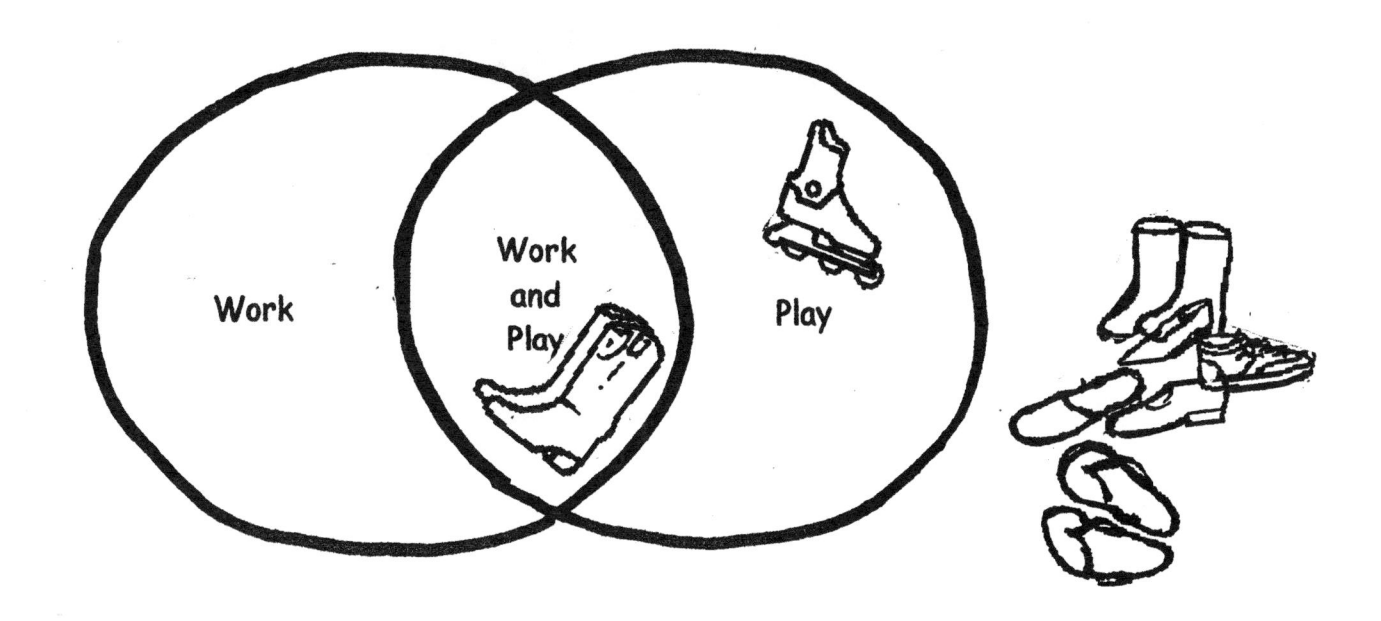

7. Collect six to eight matching pairs of shoes and a shoe-bag (see page 95). Mix up the shoes. The children find the pairs that match and then place them side-by-side in the shoe bag.

To make this activity more challenging, blind-fold the children. They will have to use only their sense of touch to match the pairs.

To make the activity more challenging, collect shoes that have similar characteristics. This will make finding a pair more difficult.

To make the activity simpler, have shoe pairs that are dissimilar; younger children will then be able to match the shoes more quickly.

8. Have the children print with shoe soles. Ask parents to send to school pairs of tennis shoes with "interesting-looking" shoe soles (it might be a great time for parents to retire some of the family's sneakers for this fun activity). You also will need butcher paper (about three feet for each child) and liquid tempera paint poured in a 9" x 13" pan. The children put the tennis shoe soles in the paint and print on the butcher paper. Encourage them to "walk" as far as they can with the tennis shoe before re-dipping it in the paint.

To make this activity more challenging, separate and group the shoe tread prints by the characteristics of the imprint. Ask the children how they would graph the results.

9. <u>Shoes, Shoes, Shoes,</u> by Ann Morris and published by Lothrop, Lee, and Shepard Books (1995), is an excellent book of photographs of many kinds of shoes, old and new: work, play, and dancing shoes. The photographs are from all over the world and the text is easy to read. Read it to the class and have it available for browsing in the Library area.

16. Where is Africa?
By Sharon MacDonald

Where is Africa?
Can you tell?
It's below Europe
Which is just as well.
'cause below Asia
Would be a mistake.
There is not enough room,
For goodness sake!

Where's Australia?
I want to know.
Is the "Land Down Under"
Above or below?
What do you think?
It's out there alone!
Knock! Knock! Knock!
Is anybody home?

North and
South America,
What's in between?
Hopefully not Antarctica--
It's not even green.
It's made of ice
And it'll freeze your nose,
And if you stay too long
It'll freeze your toes!

Activities

1. Have the children make a list of the names of continents that begin with the letter "A."

2. Find a map of the World. Place a sheet of non-adhesive interfacing (available at fabric stores) over the continents. Trace each continent, cut out and color it with colored pencils. The children match the cut out continent shapes to the ones on the World map.

3. Read the book, <u>My Map Book</u> by Sara Fanelli, published by HarperCollins. Ask the children tell you how the maps in the book are different from the maps of the United States and the World?

4. Enlarge the two continent sheets on page 98. Cut the continent silhouettes from the first sheet. The second sheet, with the names of the continents and their silhouettes, will remain intact. The children will use it as a base from which to move the continent silhouettes. To do the activity, they match the continent shape to the continent name in the poem.

Attach small pieces of hook-side *Velcro* on the back of each continent silhouette. Put the soft-side pieces of *Velcro* in the field of each continent silhouette on the second sheet (the sheet with both the continent silhouettes and the names of the continents).

Make a poster of the poem. Put soft-side Velcro pieces beside each line of the poem that has a continent name. The children remove a continent silhouette, that has been attached on sheet two and place it beside line in the poem that has the name of the continent.

Cut out the continent silhouettes on this sheet.

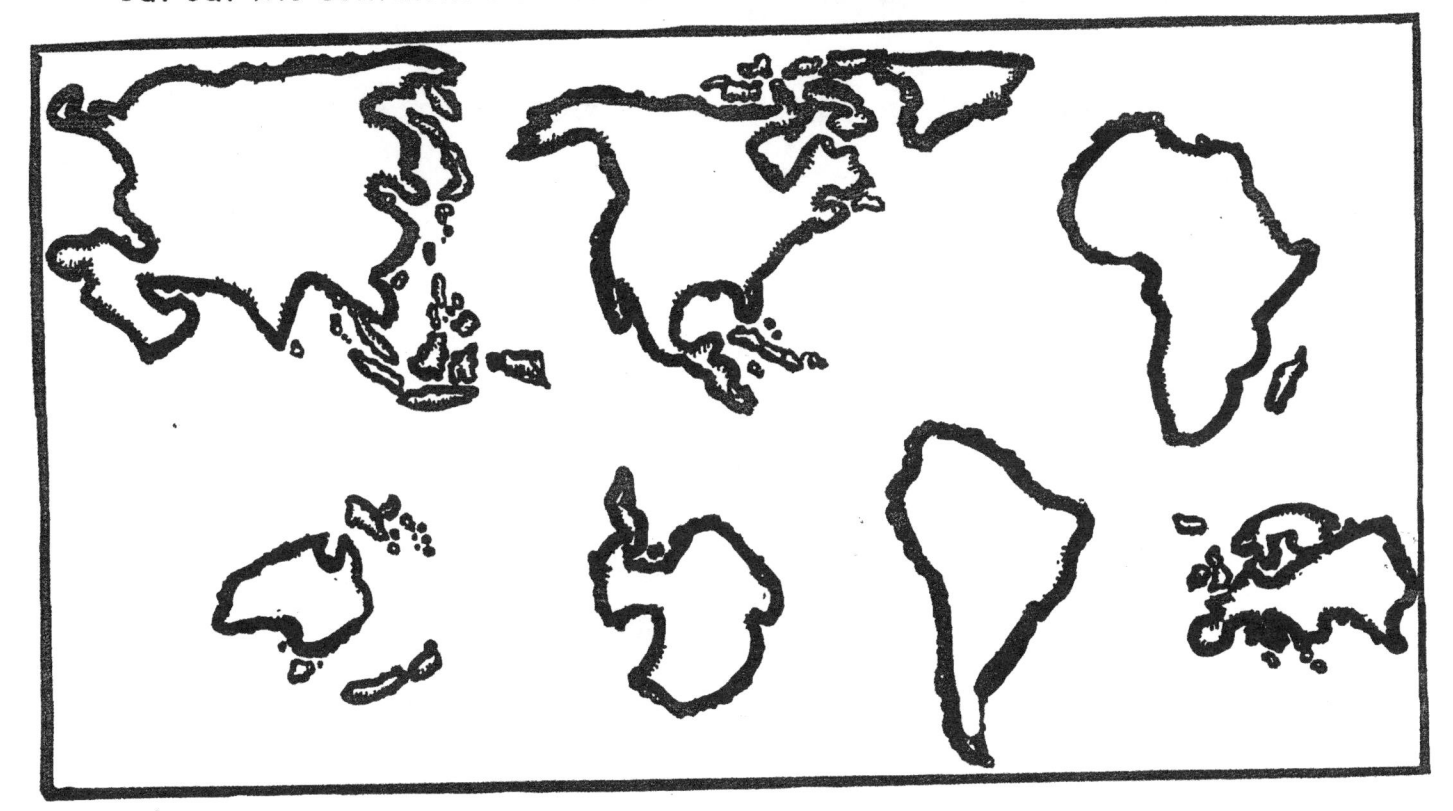

Leave the sheet below intact for the base.

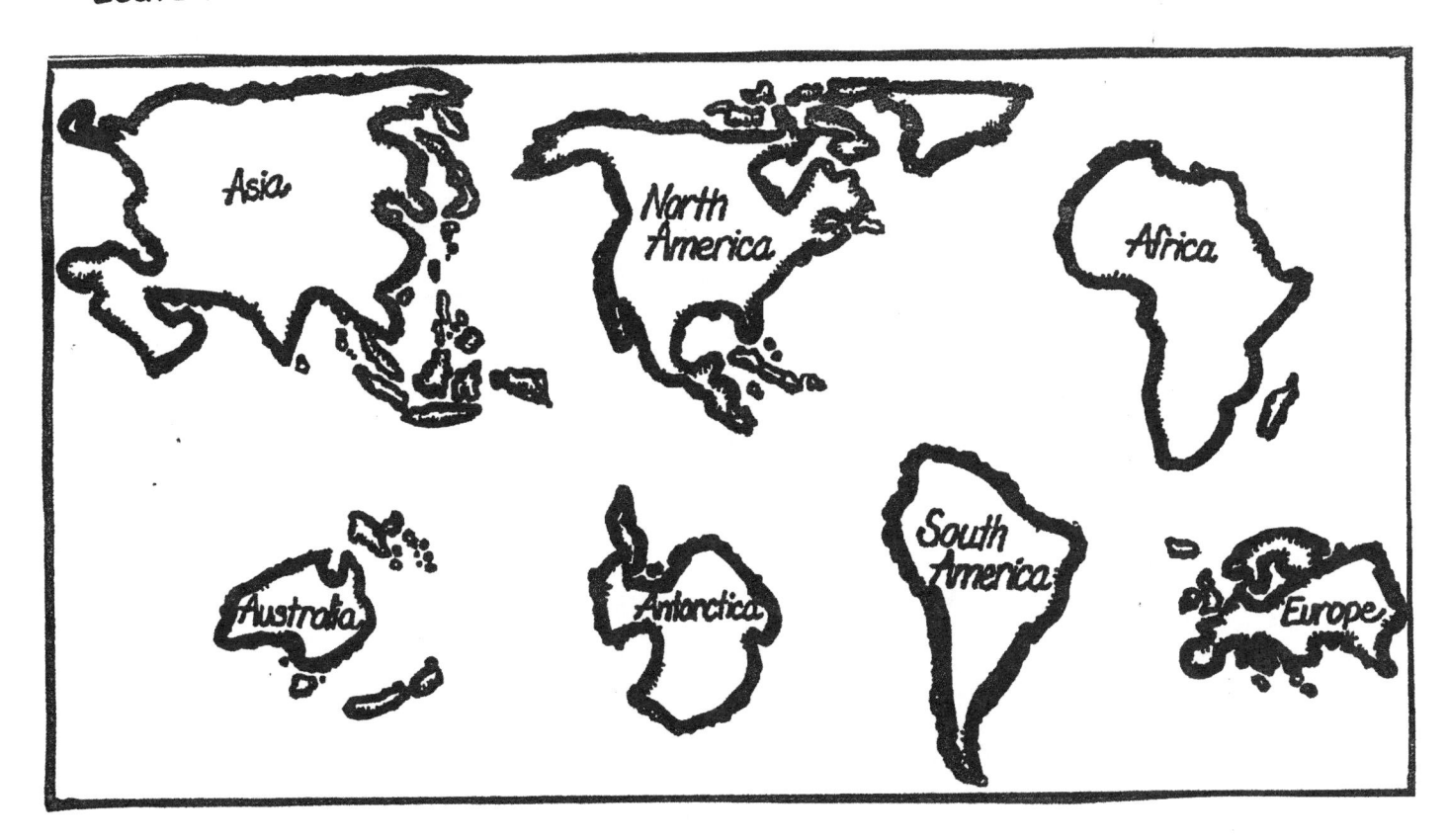

98

5. Some good resources for maps are:

- <u>Maps and Globes</u> by Jack Knowlton published by Harper Trophy.
- <u>Maps</u> by Joellyn Thrall Cicciarelli published by Creative Teaching Press.
- <u>Blank Map Outlines</u> by Instructional Fair published by TS Denison.
- You can order a "Blow-Up Globe" from the *Oriental Trading Company* catalog.
- Continent Stamps can be ordered through the Learning Zone, 10531 Gulfdale, San Antonio, TX 78216, (210) 341-4373

  (*Note: Ask for Mike; tell him Sharon sent you!*)

17. The Streamer Poem
By Sharon MacDonald

Pink, and yellow, and green, and red,
Raise your streamer when your color is said.
Orange, and blue, and purple, and white
Wave your streamer to the left and right!

Take three steps and stomp your feet.
Wave your streamer to the color beat.
Wave up high and wave down low,
Wave your streamer as you go.

Activities

1. There are eight colors mentioned in the poem. Make "leader" streamers using eight embroidery hoops. Cut 18" crepe-paper streamers and three streamers of each of the colors: pink, yellow, green, red, orange, blue, purple, and white. The streamers will be used in the embroidery hoops. Open each hoop. Lay the streamers across the inner hoop. Place the outer hoop over the inner hoop and screw them together tightly, holding the crepe paper streamers in place.

Cut more streamers 18" long. Use the colors in the poem. Give each of the remaining children their choice of a streamer. Let each child select a color. Select the children who will be the leaders to carry the hoops. Ask the children to match their color to the leader with the same color and do what their leader does as you read the poem. Let the children take turns being leaders.

2. Make a poster of the poem. Copy, color, cut out, and laminate the color squares below (they are the colors in the poem). Attach a strip of soft-side Velcro horizontally next to the first and third lines of the poem. Put a small piece of hook-side Velcro on the back of each color square. As you read the poem, the children put the color squares in the order that they occur in the poem.

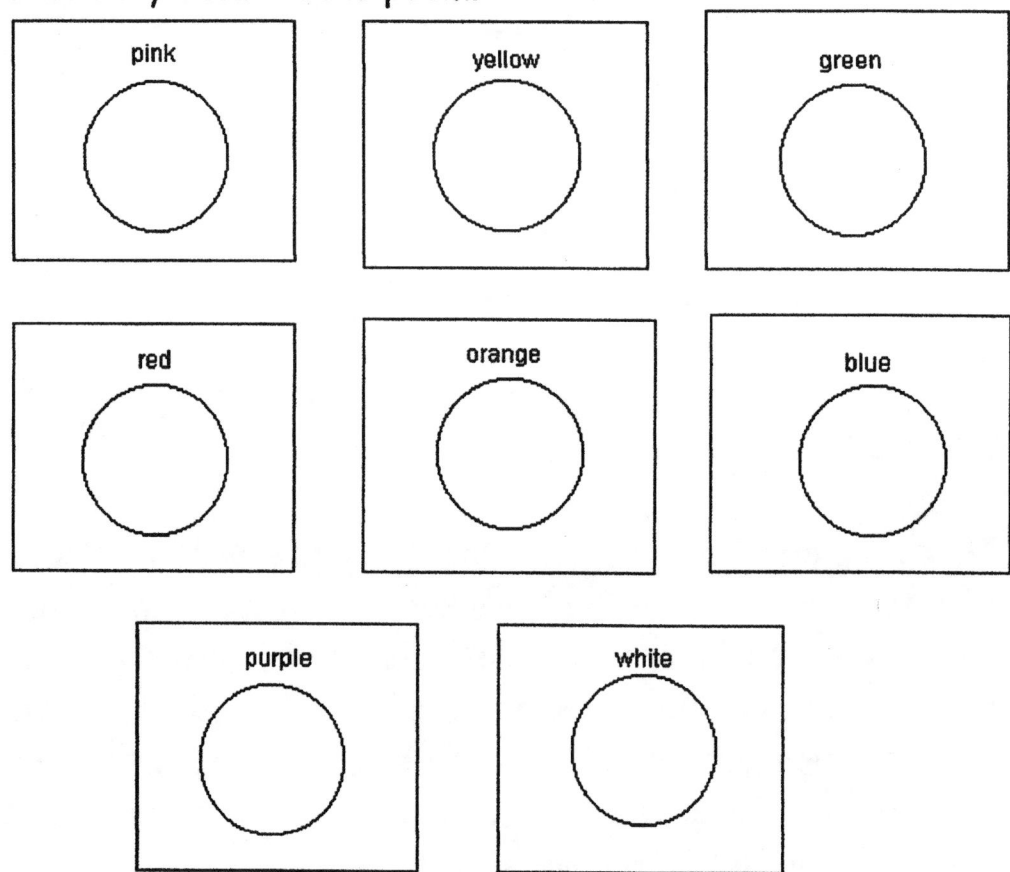

pink	yellow	green
red	orange	blue
purple	white	

Have the children re-arrange the order that the colors occur in the poem; let the children say the colors in the re-arranged order.

3. For the younger children, tie different colored crepe paper streamers to the left arms of the children and have them wave their streamer as you read the poem.